THE SEX INDUSTRY: A SURVEY OF SEX WORKERS IN QUEENSLAND, AUSTRALIA

The Sex Industry: A Survey of Sex Workers in Queensland, Australia

FRANCES M. BOYLE
SHIRLEY GLENNON
JAKE M. NAJMAN
GAVIN TURRELL
JOHN S. WESTERN
CAROLE WOOD

Routledge
Taylor & Francis Group

LONDON AND NEW YORK

First published 1997 by Ashgate Publishing

Reissued 2018 by Routledge
2 Park Square, Milton Park, Abingdon, Oxon, OX14 4RN
711 Third Avenue, New York, NY 10017, USA

Routledge is an imprint of the Taylor & Francis Group, an informa business

Copyright © F.M. Boyle, S. Glennon, J.M. Najman, G. Turrell, J.S. Western and C. Wood 1997

All rights reserved. No part of this book may be reprinted or reproduced or utilised in any form or by any electronic, mechanical, or other means, now known or hereafter invented, including photocopying and recording, or in any information storage or retrieval system, without permission in writing from the publishers.

Notice:
Product or corporate names may be trademarks or registered trademarks, and are used only for identification and explanation without intent to infringe.

Publisher's Note
The publisher has gone to great lengths to ensure the quality of this reprint but points out that some imperfections in the original copies may be apparent.

Disclaimer
The publisher has made every effort to trace copyright holders and welcomes correspondence from those they have been unable to contact.

A Library of Congress record exists under LC control number: 97070899

ISBN 13: 978-1-138-36006-8 (hbk)
ISBN 13: 978-1-138-36008-2 (pbk)
ISBN 13: 978-0-429-43333-7 (ebk)

Contents

Acknowledgements	vii
Introduction	ix
1 Social and legal perspectives	1
2 Study methods and participants	17
3 The experience of sex work	31
4 Knowledge and attitudes about safe sex practices	53
5 Sexual practices and prevention at work	69
6 Non-work risk practices	93
7 Sexual and reproductive health	105
8 Training and support needs	121
9 Contact with the police and legal system	133
10 Male sex workers	139
11 Conclusions	155
References	159

Acknowledgements

The research team acknowledges the many people who supported this study in numerous ways. Special thanks go to all those who participated in the interviews, the Management Committee, staff and members of SQWISI, the advisory committee members, the community organisations QIVAA and QUAC, the HIV/AIDS Section of Queensland Health, and Jill Pappos, Jenny Figueiredo, Zoe Gregoratos, Anna Bartos and Irene Saunderson of the Department of Anthropology and Sociology at The University of Queensland. Thanks also go to Renie Johnston for the many hours spent typing the questionnaire during the various stages of its development.

Particular acknowledgement is due to the study's research assistant who chooses to remain anonymous. She conducted the majority of the interviews and her hard work, patience, care and attention to detail, proved invaluable in ensuring the success of this research project. Thanks are due too to a second research assistant, who also remains anonymous, for conducting some of the interviews.

Introduction

This monograph presents the findings of a survey of sex industry workers in Queensland, Australia. Conducted between July 1991 and February 1992, the primary aim of the study was to investigate HIV/AIDS prevention in the sex industry. In so doing, the study sought to examine in some detail the social context of sex work, the work and non-work preventive practices of sex workers and their health-related attitudes, beliefs and behaviours.

The presented findings are based on quantitative and qualitative data derived from semi-structured interviews with 230 sex workers from a number of centres throughout Queensland. The main focus is on the 200 female workers who participated in the study, with a separate chapter devoted to the much smaller group of 28 male sex workers. Data collected from two transsexual workers are not included. None of the workers in the study sample were HIV positive according to their own self-reports. This is consistent with data from other studies indicating a low prevalence of HIV infection among Australian sex workers (Donovan, 1990; Feacham, 1995).

The social and political climate in which the study was undertaken produced certain challenges to the recruitment of workers to the study. In the aftermath of the Fitzgerald Inquiry into official corruption involving links with prostitution in Queensland, the sex industry was operating in a low key and underground manner. Strategies to enhance the participation of a large and representative sample of workers included the involvement of members of the sex workers' collective, Self-Health for Queensland Workers in the Sex Industry (SQWISI), the establishment of an Advisory Committee that included sex industry workers and the appointment of a research assistant and interviewer who had first hand experience in the sex industry. The diversity of work settings and the varied sociodemographic characteristics of the group of sex workers who participated in the study, we believe, reflects the success of these strategies.

Frequently, discussions about the sex industry and its workers start from the perspective of prostitution as a problem. 'The problem', however, is often not articulated clearly and a variety of assumptions are made about the nature of the sex industry and the 'causes' and consequences of prostitution. This study attempted to take a different starting point by avoiding, as far as possible, assumptions and judgements about prostitution. It took instead an exploratory approach which enabled the collection of information about – and, we hope, some insights into – the health and the protection and promotion of health among members of what is certainly a very diverse and complex social milieu.

While there are significant gaps in the study of prostitution, there has been a renewal of interest in the last decade. In Australia, three sex work conferences have taken place since 1988 in Melbourne, Brisbane and Canberra. These have arisen largely in response to pressures associated with both a growing movement among sex workers, feminists and others concerned with prostitution reform and reviews of prostitution laws in a number of Australian states. They have also attempted to respond to concerns (which, in the face of available data, would seem to be based far more on speculation than on fact) that sex work may be a significant vector of transmission of HIV/AIDS. More recently, Perkins, Prestage, Sharp and Lovejoy (1994) edited a multidisciplinary reader that explores and documents many of the social, legal and health contexts of the sex industry in Australia.

Plan of the book

We begin in the first chapter by examining some of the social, cultural and legal contexts that, both in the past and more recently, have helped to shape the way prostitution is thought about and managed. Considerable reference is made to proceedings from the abovementioned conferences and to the reports of the committees of inquiry held in various Australian states. Because of its obvious relevance to the socio-legal context of the present study, the chapter draws heavily on the Criminal Justice Commission Report (CJC, 1991), *Regulating Morality? An Inquiry into Prostitution in Queensland.* We then move on to the details of our study of sex workers in Queensland. In Chapter 2, we describe the background to the study and how the data were collected. Also presented are details of the sociodemographic and other background characteristics of the 200 women who participated in the study. Chapter 3 examines the kinds of settings in which women were working and also considers how and why they entered the sex industry. We see that the promise of financial returns is clearly of central importance to the women's decisions to enter and remain in the sex industry.

In Chapter 4, we begin to examine some of the issues that are more directly related to sex workers' health. We present data about the women's levels of anxiety in relation to HIV/AIDS and about their beliefs and knowledge levels in relation to a variety of potentially high-risk practices. In all, the data suggest a high level of awareness about preventive measures though some knowledge gaps clearly exist. Chapter 5 reveals the extent to which a high level of awareness about risks to health translate into effective preventive practices by exploring what sex workers actually do in their various work settings. We find that rates of reported condom use are high, but that there is no room for complacency given the prevalence of condom breakage, financial inducements from clients for non-condom sex and the special difficulties faced by more marginalised workers in relation to practicing safe sex on a consistent basis. Chapter 6 highlights an issue that is often overlooked by some discussions, namely the fact that threats to sex worker health frequently extend well beyond the arena of paid sexual encounters. Partners in the workers' private lives and the workers' own use of drugs (both legal and illegal) pose a potential threat to the health of many sex workers.

The next two chapters provide information about the workers' use of and perceived need for a variety of health and other support services. Chapter 7 outlines patterns of health service usage by the female workers and provides information about the sexual and reproductive health of this group. Chapter 8 examines some of the broader support needs of sex workers from the perspectives of both those who intend to continue working in the industry for some time and for those who wish to leave. Chapter 9 is concerned with the workers' contact with police from the point of view of a group whose members both engage in illegal activity and are exposed to threats to their physical and other safety on a regular basis. We see that violence, including rape, is a threat for most sex workers and a reality for a substantial number. Chapter 10 presents the information obtained from the 28 male sex workers who participated in the study. The clear indication is that as a group they are potentially at extremely high risk for a variety of adverse health outcomes. The final chapter, Chapter 11, reviews the findings and underlines some of the main implications arising from the study.

1 Social and legal perspectives

Any study of prostitution needs to be placed in its cultural and historical context. The aim of this chapter is to attempt to do so by reviewing overall approaches to prostitution, how it has been conceptualised and how it has been managed. In particular the legal and health responses to prostitution are examined. The focus is largely recent and on cultures similar to Australia's. Allen (1984) points out that only in recent times has prostitution been seen as an appropriate study for historians. The emphasis on local prostitution is taken largely because of the difficulties of cross-cultural comparisons where different cultures have significantly different meanings and understandings of prostitution. These issues are highlighted by Day (1988) in her anthropological analysis of prostitution and HIV in the west, Asia and sub-Saharan Africa.

What is prostitution?

While mainstream, commercial prostitution seems, at first glance to be relatively easy to define, it becomes problematic when attempting to identify the limits or the full range of what should be considered as prostitution. Legally, courts have always taken prostitution as the exchange of sexual services for monetary gain. Other forms of gain, such as temporary accommodation or food, while suggested in law, are not, in practice, equated with gain by the courts (CJC, 1991).

Survival sex, as practised by 'street kids' for example, is technically defined as prostitution. Interestingly, however, despite some effort to attract street kids to our study, none self-identified as having engaged in prostitution. This is consistent with Wilson and Arnold's (1986) study of street kids who often engage in soliciting or prostitution-like activities on an *ad hoc* basis for some time. Only some of these youth will go on to work in the formal sex industry, and only tend to identify as sex workers if this occurs. The CJC (1991) Report also points to other grey areas such as householders who may enter into an arrangement with tradespeople to exchange sexual services for goods and other services.

The suggestion then is that there may be degrees of prostitution and this argument, taken to its extreme, has seen prostitution likened to marriage:

> Marriage ... often turns into the crassest prostitution ... the wife ... differs from the ordinary courtesan only in that she does not hire out her body, like a wage earner on piece-work. but sells it into slavery once and for all. (Engels, 1973 quoted in Smart 1976:88)

Smart extended the analogy suggesting that marriage was a long term contract while the prostitute took out a series of short-lived contracts with several men. She further suggested that the significant difference between these two was not 'the number of men involved but ... sexual relations outside of marriage' (Smart, 1976:88-89).

The sale of sexual services has also been likened to other industries such as sport where players are 'bought' and 'sold' to various clubs or to situations where a person's skills are paid for:

> A woman has the right to sell sexual services just as much as she has the right to sell her brains to a law firm ... or to sell her creative work to a museum ... or to sell her image to a photographer ... or to sell her body when she works as a ballerina. Since most people can have sex without going to jail, there is no reason except old fashioned prudery to make sex for money illegal. (French, quoted in Hatty, 1991:4-5)

Consistent with this view the United States Prostitutes' Collective joined forces with the Wages for Housework movement in the early 1970s and presented prostitution as a legitimate work choice for women in a capitalist economy (Hobson, 1987). Yet, as Allen (1984) notes, many feminists would reject this comparison on the grounds that the sale of women's bodies as a sexual service to men is inherently different from the sale of other skills. It inevitably degrades the prostitute and, by her availability, women generally.

To some extent this struggle to clarify the legal definition of prostitution is the logical conclusion to a century of controversy and change around the issue of the control of women's sexuality. As noted by Hobson (1987) prostitution laws in the early 1800s in the United States were largely based on English law (as was the case in Australia). These laws were embedded in a movement around the control of the 'vicious poor' and, in particular poor women. Prostitutes were not singled out as a distinct class of deviants at this time and in linking non-marital sex with prostitution it was hoped to give all illicit sex a criminal aspect. Many other laws which sought to control women have been broken down, yet prostitution-vagrancy laws largely remain.

Part of the problem with definitions is that most work from the position that commercial prostitution is a uniform phenomenon and assume that there is a shared understanding of this phenomenon. But, prostitution for a street worker, for example, is very different from prostitution for a highly paid escort worker. Many systems which have evolved to control or regulate prostitution ignore this diversity.

The form which prostitution takes is, of course, shaped and reshaped by legal, social and criminal systems which are built around it and there continues to be a wide range of types of prostitution. Where there have been attempts to legislate for a uniform industry (e.g. Victoria with its large brothels, and Queensland with 'at home' single worker prostitution) other forms have simply continued in the illegal sphere. The legal options available must be realistic, palatable and varied enough for workers or they will be ignored by many.

Differing conceptualisations

Zajdow (1991) states that moral judgements are implicit in all discussions of prostitution but not for other forms of work (even other forms of deviant work). The construction of prostitution as problematic, and its complex relationships to morality, gender, commercial, crime and class issues, may prevent workable systems being developed around it. Questions such as those raised by Hobson (1987) as to the nature of prostitution have not been resolved. She asks if prostitution is a sexual relationship, a work contract, a private act or public commerce. How a particular society answers these questions influences the way prostitution is managed and controlled.

Solutions to 'the problem' are necessarily widely divergent. At least five major interpretations or conceptualisations of prostitution can be identified. These include prostitution as: moral decay; criminal behaviour; gender victimisation; deviance; and work. While these conceptualisations represent, to some extent, an historical progression, all continue to be presented as current and valid by various interest groups. In Queensland, this was well illustrated in public submissions to the CJC (1991), which contained elements of most of these approaches.

Prostitution as moral decay

This interpretation was most influential during the last century and was associated with growth in industrialisation and the rise of larger cities and towns of a concentrated class of poor. Most of our current laws around prostitution arise from this period, and in particular from British systems.

Prostitution was associated with poverty and vagrancy, and hence, laws around it became embedded in vagrancy laws. It was not really separated as a criminal activity at this time. There was also a lack of differentiation between poor women, 'fallen women', women in *de facto* relationships, mistresses and prostitutes (Hobson, 1987).

Many writers have stressed the inherent double standard in this treatment of women. The 'Madonna/Whore' dichotomy divides women into two types: those 'good' women who marry or remain celibate and who are generally seen as asexual and 'bad', sexually active women who are generally represented as prostitutes. This class of 'bad' women was necessary to ensure males had access to sexual gratification while at the same time maintaining the facade of morality. Smart (1976:84) notes that this implies that 'promiscuous females are unnatural and problematic while males cannot be promiscuous because their sexual drive is "naturally" irrepressible and fairly indiscriminate.' Hobson (1987) also points out that, even during the most repressive anti-vice campaigns, prostitution areas continued to flourish, always within easy reach of business and city districts.

Prostitution as criminal behaviour

As described by a number of authors the categorisation of prostitution as criminal is closely related to the complexity and 'respectability' of a particular society. Hobson traces this in San Francisco:

> San Francisco prostitutes in the frontier years ... were respected and admired, politely mentioned in the press, and welcomed to meetings at the schoolhouse. But in the next decade, as more families moved to San Francisco, law enforcers designated a zone for prostitutes, the Barbary Coast. Respectable folk would not have to be offended by a prostitute's soliciting or by the presence of brothels near their homes. Police ignored discreet high class brothels in residential neighbourhoods; but contacts with prostitutes had to be made on the sly because the prostitute, even the elegant courtesan or madam, was beyond the social pale. (Hobson, 1987:25-6)

In Australia, historical analyses of New South Wales by Anne Summers (1975) and Judith Allen (1984) suggest that most women in the early days of Australian settlement were subject to an 'enforced whoredom' because of lack of employment and a shortage of women. As Sydney became the focus of free settlement, however, women increasingly became divided into 'good' and 'bad'. It was at this time that criminalisation of prostitution began to be enforced. As Allen (1984) points out, this forced women to seek invisibility and protection from criminal organisations, leading them to lose any power they had as independent sex workers.

A similar pragmatism in the face of a shortage of women comes from this century. In Brisbane during World War II, Moore (CJC, 1991) reports that the then Prime Minister, John Curtin became concerned at the ability to keep the peace in Brisbane with quarter of a million American servicemen stationed there. According to Moore, a Sydney underworld figure was approached by federal authorities and duly arranged for a train load of prostitutes to be sent from Sydney to Brisbane. Post-war, however, this had no long term effect or improvement on the position of prostitutes.

The criminalisation of prostitution then, has its roots partly in moral arguments and partly in class and commercial interest which come to predominate at certain periods of a society's development. Criminalisation, however, brings with it a range of dilemmas and paradoxes. Hobson traces the rise of small business reformers in a number of American cities in the 1830s-1850s who were elected on an anti-prostitution platform. They were unable to achieve their election promises, however, due to powerful vested interests and the loss of faith of the working classes. These groups did not want prostitution in their neighbourhoods but were unwilling to bear the tax burden of heavy enforcement of anti-prostitution laws (Hobson, 1987). As many sources have identified, police and courts do not tend to actively devote resources to enforcing prostitution laws unless there is pressure for them to do so. They tend to 'contain' or move prostitution activity to areas or types of activity which will gain little attention (Hobson, 1987; CJC, 1991; Victorian Inquiry into Prostitution, 1985). Hobson summarises the effects of the laws as follows:

> A policeman on his rounds, when he plucked the flower on the streets, rarely took the stem or branches, and the system never touched the roots. Law enforcers went after the easiest and most visible target, the public prostitute, they often ignored the keeper, almost always passed over the clients, and never adopted measures that touched the social and economic causes of prostitution. (Hobson, 1987:48)

The regulatory body, rather than the law, in effect becomes the arbiter of what is and what is not acceptable in terms of prostitution. A logical consequence of this pragmatic policing approach is the potential for corruption. An historical analysis of prostitution in Queensland by the CJC (1991) points out that, for much of this century, Queensland was significantly different from New South Wales in this respect. There was no organised crime syndicate in the 1920s in Queensland in relation to prostitution. Also, until 1959 two authorities (health and police) through the Contagious Diseases Act 1886, had joint responsibility for the regulation of prostitution. This seems to have contributed to limiting the possibilities for systematic corruption.

Prior to 1980 the CJC report suggests that, while corruption in relation to prostitution existed in Queensland it was 'opportunistic corruption' and it was not until the early 1980s that systematic corruption emerged. It was at this time that a number of factors, which were prerequisites for organised criminals to flourish, were in evidence. These included a consolidation of control of illegal activities, the integration of prostitution with other criminal activities and substantial modification of the regulatory environment (CJC, 1991).

Current arguments for not decriminalising prostitution in Queensland include the nexus with organised crime and the impossibility of breaking this nexus. The CJC reports that this nexus is now largely broken. Given that this is an acknowledged problem common to other areas (racing and gambling for example) it seems that the reluctance to deal with prostitution stems from other concerns.

The existence of prostitution does not automatically imply the existence of corruption, although where considerable consolidation has occurred in an illegal industry it is more likely and unless the internal culture of the law enforcement body is strongly resistant, it may be successful (CJC, 1991). The issue of whether the criminal system should be used to enforce public morality (in particular, to reflect Christian morality) is important in this context. While many support this role for the law, public attitude surveys conducted under the auspices of the CJC did not suggest that the public in general view prostitution as immoral.

Gender victimisation

Gender victimisation provides the basis for feminist analyses of prostitution. Prostitution has been widely recognised as one of the clearest examples of women's structural inequality and lack of access to economic and political power. However, while most feminist analyses begin here, there are a number of points at which they diverge. This reflects the range of perspectives on prostitution within the feminist movement itself.

Historically, gender victimisation has its roots in the moral reform movements of last century. These movements were largely made up of women and they espoused the prostitute's cause on the basis of gender consciousness. One of the most significant concepts to emerge from this movement was the notion of 'forced choice'. Hobson (1987:5) suggests that 'middle class reformers could not grasp the motivations, moral codes, and survival strategies of poor women ... that prostitution could appear as a viable alternative to low wages and lack of employment options'. Protection, rather than punishment, was the goal of these groups and according to Hobson this translated into the imposition of strong controls on most aspects of young women's lives and not the punishment of exploitative males.

Most prostitute and feminist groups today reject the notion of absolute coercion evident in this approach. However, some groups such as *WHISPER* (Women Hurt In Systems of Prostitution Engaged in Revolt) in the United Sates continue to present a perspective which seems to support this. Similarly, one women's electoral lobby group, in its submission to the CJC, consistently portrayed workers principally as victims (CJC, 1991). Hobson (1987) sees prostitutes neither as passive victims nor as heroic rebels rejecting social conventions. Structural inequalities, however continue to create social conditions whereby the choice to engage in sex work will be an issue for some groups of women and not others.

Hatty (1991) suggests that being a member of a marginalised group, as in the case of poor, immigrant, and rural women, increases vulnerability to recruitment into prostitution. In Australia, while most mainstream workers would consider their choice to be voluntary (CJC, 1991; Victorian Inquiry, 1985; the present study), the issue of Asian workers needs to be considered. Here the issue of forced choice is more pressing and powerful than for many Australian workers. The CJC report notes that in southern states of Australia it is common for Asian women to be imported for periods of time to work in the sex industry. They have little independence, few choices in their work settings and little protection in terms of violence or health. The CJC notes its concern about this and suggests that, while it does not occur on a large scale currently in Queensland, the potential is there (CJC, 1991). It is a repetition at an international level of the exploitation possible in prostitution at an individual level.

Prostitutes themselves had no voice in these debates until the 1970s. Where women's reformist groups were supportive of change in the past, prostitutes were not involved in the process. Even today much of the feminist thought on the subject is purely theoretical and there has been little involvement of sex workers (Banach, 1992). Many feminists have become uneasy advocates of prostitution reform and yet frequently find themselves at odds with workers themselves. Hobson (1987:220) suggests that 'curiously, sexual liberation has had the dual effect of breaking down many of the social barriers between prostitutes and straight women while constructing ideological barriers between them'.

Deviance

Neave (1988) suggests that until relatively recently most research on prostitution concentrated almost exclusively on the personal and social background of those who sold sexual services and largely ignored significant social and economic factors. She suggests that prostitutes were categorised as deviant because they did not fit the usual stereotype of 'passive, monogamous and faithful'. In contrast, client behaviour was seen as normal. Smart (1976) traces the development of a number of deviant interpretations of prostitutes. Early criminal theorists suggested that prostitutes were 'primitive' and 'uncivilised'. It was later concluded that the prostitute, because of her apparently indiscriminate sexual behaviour was over-sexed. Havelock Ellis, in the 1930s, however, developed the view that prostitutes were actually sexually frigid and/or homosexual. A range of Freudian and neo-Freudian theories followed. Prostitutes were said to have psychopathological defects, the problem being viewed as an individual not a social one. Smart (1976) suggests that the significant outcome of the location of the problem with the woman is that she becomes the cause of the problem and may be justifiably punished, treated or protected.

Currently workers may be subject to a different type of deviant label. One prostitute group, in particular, in the United States differs markedly from other groups and has no comparable voice among workers in Australia. This group is *WHISPER* and its beliefs correspond closely to a sexual politics analysis of prostitution as institutionalised male violence directed at all women. Hunter (1991) suggests that:

> In response to other sex worker groups in the United Sates, *WHISPER* often states that working in the sex industry is so damaging that sex workers who say they aren't damaged are simply internalising that damage, or that they are brainwashed by the patriarchy into believing that sex work is good, because it suits men that way. (Hunter, 1991:3)

His criticism of such a position is that it fails to deal with the issue of consent and like many earlier analyses of prostitution portrays women purely as victims.

Similarly, some such as Seng (1989), have suggested that child sexual abuse is a significant precursor to prostitution. Other studies, including Perkins (1994) and our own, however, have not revealed unusually high rates of abuse among workers. This is an area which requires further, careful analysis before any conclusions can be drawn about sexual abuse as a predisposing factor for prostitution. Other studies have examined a range of individual characteritstics, including the personality of the women (or men) involved. While providing useful data, it is important that these analyses be viewed in the context of a broader social understanding of prostitution.

Prostitution as work

Following trends in the United States and Canada, Australian prostitute advocacy groups adopted the approach of prostitution as sex work in the mid to late 1980s. Hunter (1991) suggests that the term 'sex work' was first used in Australia to avoid the stigma associated with other terms for prostitution. This conceptualisation continues to incite outrage and protest from groups representing a wide range of perspectives. The CJC (1991) noted a number of objections to its use of the term in its report. In Australia however, there has been considerable feminist support for the use of the term 'sex work'.

Sullivan (1991:4) argues that the Australian feminist position has been somewhat different from that of overseas feminists in that early significant works such as *Dammed Whores and God's Police* (Summers, 1975) led to a recognition of 'connections rather than traditional distinctions between marriage and sex work'. She notes that strong links were forged in Australia in the 1970s between feminists and prostitute advocacy groups and that the prostitution as work concept became a key feature of these links.

Sullivan (1991) also adds some criticisms of the term 'sex worker'. The term does not, for example, distinguish between the range of types of sex work and circumstances or the types of workers. More importantly it leaves the primary object of analysis as the worker and allows the client to remain largely invisible.

'Prostitution minimisation'

This position is best explained by Neave (1988) who outlines four key principles for appropriate reform in the area. Overall, prostitution minimisation is an attempt to reconcile and synthesise the gender victimisation and the prostitution as work interpretations of prostitution.

The first of the four principles is the recognition that prostitution is based on the inequality of women. Neave asserts that prostitution should not be seen as an inevitable male entitlement and that prostitution will only decrease (or vanish) when women gain real economic and political power. Rejection of the inevitability of prostitution (even in the very long term) is significant in policy terms and precludes the institutionalisation of government-endorsed prostitution. At the same time it implies that other issues such as the commodification of women generally must be addressed.

The immediate issue then becomes the management of the current problems associated with prostitution, such as costs to the community and individuals, official corruption, uneven enforcement, and lack of civil and industrial rights of individuals. Neave's next two principles attempt to deal with these issues.

The second principle is the repeal of criminal laws around prostitution and its associated activities. She argues that 'criminal penalties should only exist to protect adult prostitutes from coercion and fraud and to protect young people from sexual exploitation'. Loitering and soliciting, where they cause public nuisance, can be dealt with under general public nuisance provisions. Living off the earnings provisions date back to a nineteenth century view that even adult women needed protection from predatory males and are no longer relevant. Indeed they may inhibit a sex worker's freedom to form supportive and loving relationships.

Thirdly, laws developed around the business of prostitution should empower prostitutes. They should have control over aspects of their work such as choice of clients, health issues, safety of work and ability to work independently.

The final principle concerns controlling those aspects of prostitution which the community does find offensive. Neave acknowledges that some venues, such as large brothels, can become a focus for offensive and noisy behaviour. She states, however, that specific laws relating to brothels are not required and that existing offensive behaviour and town planning laws are sufficient to manage these problems.

The key area of conflict between the position that prostitution is work and prostitution minimisation is in the ideological assumption that prostitution will vanish in a society where men and women are equal. Sex worker groups and advocates suggest that this is a naive and fairly one-dimensional view and misunderstands the nature of prostitution. Minimisation focuses almost solely on the gender aspects of prostitution and ignores the class, sexual and commercial bases of the industry. It comes from an idealised view of sexual exchanges. Inherent in the argument seems to be a notion that sexual exchanges should take place within an exclusive, semi-permanent, private and non-commercial relationship. It also ignores the potential of the sex industry to change its nature (not just its form or organisation) with changing social and sexual mores.

Qualitative information from our study suggests that prostitution today is not the 'rite of passage' it once was for males. It was once relatively common for a young male's first sexual experience to have been with a sex worker. It is now more likely to be a girlfriend. Workers report that their clientele today is generally older and more likely to be married or to have been married than was the case in the past. Tourism and business also provide more clients. Demand seems to have become situational rather than regular or ritualised as it once seemed to be. Although comparisons between studies of sexuality are fraught with problems it is interesting to note that Kinsey and colleagues, researching in the United States in the 1940s and 1950s found that 69 per cent of the white male population had ever visited a prostitute (Kinsey, Pomeroy and Martin, 1948) whereas a study commissioned by the Queensland Department of Health in 1988 found that only 25 per cent of males had ever done so (Wilson, 1988). The report of prostitution in the Australian Capital Territory (ACT Select Committee, 1991) supports the view that the current exploitation of women in prostitution is more to do with social conditions and power relationships than biological differences. Women's sexual needs are less likely to be expressed, while men are more likely to conform to social norms and expectations. Changes in power relationships likely to accompany genuine equality for women may also affect the demand for prostitution services in ways different from those suggested. More women may demand prostitution services of some kind or, as already foreshadowed in the exploitation of Asian workers in Australia, developed nations may look to third world countries for sex workers.

Legal responses to prostitution

There are many differences in terminology used to describe legal systems applied to prostitution. This is partly due to the difficulty of categorising the often quite idiosyncratic responses of particular legislative bodies at certain periods of time. Some sex worker groups refuse to discuss terms such as legalisation or decriminalisation because of automatic assumptions made as to their meaning. In Australia, for example, legalisation is commonly equated with the system in Victoria. This system, however, is not representative of legalised systems and is only a partial implementation of the legalised system recommended by the Neave Inquiry (Neave, 1988) in that state. The four major systems frequently identified are: abolition, suppression, legalisation and decriminalisation (Banach, 1992). Given problems with the comprehensiveness of this terminology, however, and some confusion as to their meanings it is also fruitful to add 'regulation' (CJC, 1991) and 'decriminalisation with controls' (Collaery, 1991).

Abolition

Abolition refers to systems where prostitution itself is not illegal but most activities around it are. This was and to some extent still is the case in Queensland. Effectively it criminalises sex workers and others involved in the industry. Its aim is to ensure the public face of respectability is maintained.

Suppression

Suppression criminalises the act of prostitution itself and its aim is total eradication. In Queensland currently the system is an odd mix of abolition and suppression (Banach, 1992). Prostitution remains legal under the very limited circumstances of one worker working from home and other activities are illegal (abolition). All other types of prostitution and related activities have been defined as illegal (suppression). Many authors and inquiries have reported on the lack of efficacy of either abolition or suppression (Neave, 1988; Victorian Inquiry, 1985; ACT Select Committee, 1991; Hobson, 1987; CJC, 1991).

Hatty (1991) reports on an evaluation of Canadian legislation introduced to decrease street solicitation, the keeping of houses of prostitution, procuring prostitutes for others and under-age prostitution, and an attempt to ensure that the law was equally applied to male and female prostitutes and their customers. The evaluation revealed that street solicitation was not decreased but simply displaced to other parts of the cities involved, the working conditions and vulnerability of the street workers increased, the tendency to prosecute workers rather than clients or managers continued, and the sentences received by prostitutes were more severe than those received by their clients (even allowing for previous criminal records).

Legalisation

As pointed out in the CJC (1991) Report there is considerable confusion around this term. Commissioner Fitzgerald viewed legalisation as a state whereby the activities were no longer regulated in any way. In contrast, the New South Wales Select Committee, and the more common definition, views legalisation as the state whereby the activities are legal but are accompanied by regulation (CJC, 1991).

Decriminalisation

This is the option preferred by most sex worker groups. It involves the removal of criminal penalties from all aspects of adult, voluntary prostitution and the management of the industry through business codes, public nuisance laws and town planning laws.

Regulation

It is important to separate out regulated systems because they often evolve within other systems. Regulated systems are those which, no matter what the legal framework, effectively tolerate and contain prostitution within limits usually defined by police or other regulatory bodies. Currently Western Australia and Nevada are often cited examples of regulation or containment.

In Queensland, tacit regulation was established between 1870 and 1911, lasting until 1959. The CJC Report (1991) states that until then prostitution was relatively immune to organised crime. This is not to suggest that it was necessarily a preferable working environment for workers themselves. Anderson (1991) from interviews with women who worked in Queensland at the time gives the following description:

> Two workers at the time were taken away on suspicion of having an infectious disease. They were detained in the 'Lock' Hospital at Bogga Road ... while there they were given weekly health checks. During their incarceration they climbed a ten foot wall and ran away. They were apprehended and sent to Bogga Road jail for three months ... Neither had any diseases. It could be argued that women such as the street workers simply became too independent by hiring their own rooms and breaking out of the stereotype of the time. In the 'houses' of the time ... the worker would live on the premises and stay there for various periods of time. A cleaner maintained these houses and their meals were provided. They were only allowed to go into the town to do their personal shopping, sometimes only in the company of the madam, and if they went drinking late at night they were forbidden to mix with any of the menfolk. In most of these tolerated brothels workers were not allowed to have boyfriends. Boyfriends would have threatened accessibility by clients and would also perhaps have threatened the control which the police exercised at the time. (Anderson 1991:3)

Despite the excessive deprivation of rights and control over workers within this system, the closure of these regulated or tolerated brothels in 1959 was not to signal improvements for workers. The closure was, in fact, associated with the precursors of organised crime. A significant change was the shifting of responsibility for the Vagrancy Act to the Licensing Branch in Queensland, which was already corrupt in relation to SP bookmaking, and the removal of the health department from involvement in the regulation of the industry (CJC, 1991).

As the houses closed, workers moved to hotel lounges and inner city flats and, as in New South Wales had a higher need for invisibility and protection. They became more directly involved in other criminal activity and in individual corrupt arrangements with police.

Decriminalisation with controls

There have also been calls for 'decriminalisation with controls'. This may be because of the confusion over terminology as already discussed or because of a reluctance of the state to be seen to be somehow condoning prostitution, through involvement in its regulation. Collaery (1991) sees decriminalisation with controls as being an effective middle ground between decriminalisation and legalisation and it was recommended by the Australian Capital Territory Select Committee on HIV, Prostitution, and Illegal Drugs (1991).

The CJC (1991) also avoided the terminology debate and summarised possible options under four headings: strict enforcement of the criminal law; no application of the criminal law; partial application of the criminal law; and, regulation of prostitution-related activities by means other than the criminal law.

Hobson (1987) notes that there is a false dichotomy between tolerant and intolerant systems. Both are similar in intent and consequences for workers. Regulation (or so called 'tolerant' systems) defines, confines, controls and curtails most aspects of workers' lives. Seemingly oppressive systems, however, having to work within the law and without the extensive powers of the regulatory bodies were actually associated with more open and flexible prostitution markets.

Health responses to prostitution

Government agencies responsible for health traditionally have been very involved in the control of prostitution, usually under the guise of control of sexually transmitted disease. Allen (1984) suggests that the debate in Europe, America and Australia during the second half of the nineteenth century about the relationship of prostitution, medicine, morality and the state was significant in establishing the framework within which prostitution developed in New South Wales.

The spread of disease (or the fear of spread of disease) has been used as a powerful means of social control. In Queensland the Contagious Diseases Act of 1886 was used for much of this century within the semi-regulated system operating until 1959 and previous examples from Anderson (1991) demonstrate its power to restrict and curtail prostitutes' lives.

There is now a similar situation in relation to HIV/AIDS. There is a continued and largely unwarranted emphasis on workers rather than clients, workers rather than partners and sex workers rather than very sexually active non-workers as vectors of transmission of the virus. This occurs despite the fact that a number of studies and inquiries have concluded along with the Australian Capital Territory Select Committee on HIV, Illegal Drugs and Prostitution (1991:26), 'that the link between HIV infection of the general community and prostitution has not been substantiated'. Despite this lack of substantiation, the link has been used to scapegoat a marginalised group in the community (prostitutes) whilst tacitly ignoring the role and responsibilities of the dominant group (clients).

This is not to suggest that government health agencies themselves are always in favour of the criminalisation of prostitution. The Queensland Health submission to the CJC Inquiry generally supported a legalised, open system and was opposed to the compulsory testing of workers. It was of the opinion that such systems enabled ease of access and cooperation with the industry, which ultimately was more productive in health terms than systems which forced workers underground and made them distrustful of any government agency (CJC, 1991). The CJC survey of public attitudes to prostitution, in contrast, found that while the majority of respondents generally supported some relaxation of the current law, the issue of greatest concern to them in relation to prostitution was the spread of STDs and AIDS (CJC, 1991). The potential remains, given the extensive powers still available to Queensland Health under the Health Act in relation to notifiable diseases, for public opinion to pressure health officials to use these powers inappropriately.

The current situation in Queensland

The changes made to Queensland law following the CJC Report have proved to be a tightening rather than a relaxation of the situation for workers. The only form of legal work for sex workers is that of working alone from their own home. The effect of this is that private work (as defined in Chapter 3 of this report) is now the predominant type of work in Queensland. The majority of female sex workers now work on their own, with some working together in split shifts. A smaller number of escort agencies still operate, with street work being at a similar level as that reported in the study (personal communication with SQWISI representatives).

One of the most significant aspects of the current legislation is that it takes the sex worker out of the sphere of work. The effect of making the only legal form of work for prostitutes that of working alone from home has been to render most workers more vulnerable and more isolated. Of particular concern are younger, inexperienced workers, those in regional areas of Queensland and others who are less likely to be involved in industry networks.

For many workers the separation of home and work allows for a concept of professionalisation in relation to sex work. The new legislation harks back to Victorian times in its effect of forcing a reamalgamation of home and work life for prostitutes. The woman is first and foremost a prostitute before she is a worker, mother, spouse or member of the community. Restrictive conditions such as these are unheard of for any other form of work. It echoes previous legislation where a woman could be arrested simply for being a prostitute. Given the conceptualisations of prostitution discussed earlier in this chapter this approach may best be described as moral decay masquerading as gender victimisation. The fact that a health and welfare package was associated with the introduction of a quite repressive system suggests that the notion of protection of women and control of their lives is fundamental to the thinking behind the changes.

Justification for these changes has been around a number of issues: a sexual politics feminist position that prostitution is inherently exploitative of women; the equation of legalised prostitution with the system operating currently in Victoria; and the view that organised crime and drugs will always be associated with prostitution. Most feminists, however, who hold that prostitution is undesirable and exploitative do not advocate its criminalisation. This position also fails to recognise that prostitutes very frequently exercise control over the sexual exchange and that exploitation within criminalised systems, from police, managers, clients and in civil liberties terms can be much worse for workers. Neave (1988) has consistently pointed out that the system in Victoria is only a partial implementation of the recommendations of her inquiry. The history of prostitution in Queensland itself demonstrates that prostitution can operate without the involvement of organised crime and, as pointed out by the CJC Inquiry, this nexus was successfully broken post-Fitzgerald (CJC, 1991).

Summary

Prostitution, the way it is conceived by society, the laws around it and the responses to those laws are developed and influenced by a large number of factors. Gender, class, religious beliefs. commerce, crime, health, law, sexuality, social norms, and beliefs about public and private spheres of life all produce pressures which in many cases are oppositional and make genuine reform of prostitution difficult and politically unpopular. Hobson (1987:3) maintains that 'prostitution will always lead into a moral quagmire in democratic societies with capitalist economies; it invades the terrain of intimate sexual relations yet beckons for regulation'. In Queensland and elsewhere in Australia, the outcome of attempts at reform has been to undertake superficial reforms aimed at one section of the industry while failing to implement full and systematic reform. The consequence of this failure to deal seriously with the problems associated with prostitution is to produce a facade of conservative morality while at the same time acknowledging the inevitability and easy availability of prostitution.

2 Study methods and participants

The following chapters of this report summarise our investigation of a range of issues relating to the sex industry in Queensland, Australia, with particular emphasis on the prevention of HIV infection. The main focus is on female sex workers because the number of male sex workers who participated in the study was too small to allow meaningful conclusions to be drawn. However, a separate chapter is devoted to the 28 male sex workers who did participate in the study. As others have noted (Prestage, 1994), their experience of sex work tends to differ markedly from that of female sex workers.

The research sought to describe the social background, work practices and health-related risk behaviours characteristic of the sex industry in Queensland between July 1991 and February 1992. At this time there was virtually no information about the sex industry in Queensland other than that which was anecdotally available from some sex workers. Research was required to provide baseline data on HIV risk-related issues and to inform prevention programs which were in the early stages of development at the time.

The main aims of the study were to:

- develop a profile of the sex industry in Queensland, based on demographic and other social background data;
- describe the range of work settings by drawing on workers' own perceptions of the sex industry;
- investigate HIV-related attitudes and knowledge of sex workers;
- determine the level and range of HIV-related preventive practices used by sex workers in both their work and private lives;
- investigate the extent of violence and sexual abuse suffered by sex workers and their level of involvement with police; and
- examine the support, education and information needs of sex workers.

Background to the study

The project was conducted by the Department of Anthropology and Sociology at The University of Queensland with initial project support from the Queensland Department of Health (Queensland Health). It was funded by a Commonwealth AIDS Research Grant. At the time of planning and establishing the research in Queensland, the CJC review of prostitution, discussed in the previous chapter, was in progress. An AIDS prevention program had been established by the State Health Department in 1989, with the community organisation SQWISI being established under the National HIV/AIDS Strategy to outreach and educate Queensland sex industry workers about preventive practices.

In the aftermath of the Fitzgerald Inquiry into official corruption in Queensland involving links with prostitution, the sex industry was operating in a low key and underground manner. Before the Fitzgerald Inquiry, massage parlours operated openly, under an unofficial police policy of tolerance. During this period many workers attended the public STD clinics, as most parlours operated a policy which required employees to undergo regular medical checks. Attendance at the STD clinic in Brisbane is reported to have fallen dramatically during the Fitzgerald Inquiry, due to the impact of increased media attention and because of a change to more restrictive legislation and policing. The opportunity for contact with health professionals, who could monitor the prevalence of STDs and HIV, was therefore limited at this time.

During the data collection phase (July 1991 to February 1992), a greater number of brothels had begun operating in a climate of increased confidence about law reform and uncertain policies on the regulation of prostitution. Escort agencies, private solo workers, and street workers were also known to be operating. However, during the course of the study, the dimensions, location and nature of the sex industry underwent significant change in response to prevailing social and political forces. The more recent legislation, essentially restricting sex workers to single owner-operator settings, has resulted in further changes but these have not yet been thoroughly documented.

Health risks associated with sex work

The connection between commercial sex and STDs has been the subject of a considerable amount of research (see, for example, Estebanez, Fitch and Najera, 1993; Harcourt, 1994; Jackson, Highcrust and Coates, 1992; Plant, 1990). The risk for sex workers of becoming infected with HIV is potentially high given their exposure to numerous sex partners. Among sex workers who use intravenous drugs, there is also potential for transmission if needles and syringes are shared. Among those reports of HIV infection in women who have ever worked in prostitution, intravenous drug use seems to be the major risk factor (Estebanez, Fitch and Najera, 1993; Harcourt, 1994). The prevalence of HIV infection among female sex workers in Australia is very low and, among those identified as HIV positive, injection drug use has been established as the most likely source of infection (Donovan, 1990). As Harcourt (1994) points out, there is no documented case of a female sex worker in Australia either receiving or transmitting HIV infection through sexual relations with a client. Men who work in the sex industry have been less frequently studied than women. However, the indication is that HIV prevalence is higher among men than among women in the industry (Plant, 1990; Feacham, 1995; Elifson, Boles and Sweat, 1993; Estebanez, Fitch and Najera, 1993; Griggs and Alan, 1990).

Methods

The initial stage of the research project involved consultation with a wide range of agencies and individuals and a review of the relevant literature. Efforts were made to enlist support from SQWISI (who had already identified the need for comprehensive research of the sex industry in Queensland), and other key groups and individuals in the community. The Research Division of the CJC was also consulted in the early stages of the project.

Advisory Committee

A number of sex workers who expressed an early interest in participating in the study were invited to become members of an Advisory Committee to oversee the project. The Committee comprised of a range of people representing different groups working in the sex industry in Queensland. Direction was sought from the Advisory Committee on all major aspects of the research, including the design and content of the survey questionnaire, the development of a position description for the study's research assistant, sampling issues, and the dissemination of the research findings.

Key informants

Two of the investigators who were connected with SQWISI as health professionals began the research by conducting taped interviews with a small number of sex workers. These key informant studies enabled the identification of a range of issues and provided guidance for the development of the questionnaire for use in the quantitative phase of the research.

Eighteen in-depth interviews were conducted, with the sample chosen to reflect different aspects of prostitution. Most of these initial respondents were personally known to the interviewers through their involvement in SQWISI. Five workers also came forward in response to an advertisement in SQWISI's magazine, the *Hookers Herald* (now *RESPECT*).

The interviews were guided by a short schedule of open-ended questions covering a wide range of topics identified from the literature and by the Advisory Committee as being potentially relevant to the study objectives. The schedule served as a prompt to ensure coverage of the full range of identified issues. Open-ended questions were included to encourage respondents to provide as much detail as possible. The transcribed interviews formed the basis for qualitative perspectives which accompany, illustrate and elucidate survey data presented in this report.

Following the key informant interviews, a research assistant who had experience in the sex industry was appointed to work full-time on the project. She conducted all but twenty of the structured interviews. The remaining interviews were conducted by a second research assistant who had also worked in the sex industry and who was employed on this project on a contractual basis.

Questionnaire development

A structured questionnaire was developed from the topics which emerged from the above interviews. The questionnaire covered a wide range of areas including:

- type of work and work history;
- knowledge and attitudes about HIV transmission;
- licensing issues, relations with police, industry profile;
- sexual and drug-related preventive practices at work and in private life;
- alcohol and drug use;
- service use and sexual health;
- education, training and support issues; and
- demographic information.

The General Health Questionnaire (GHQ-28; Goldberg and Williams, 1988), a self-report measure of psychological state covering recent somatic symptoms, anxiety, insomnia, social dysfunction and depression was also completed by workers who participated in the survey. The results of this component of the survey are detailed elsewhere (Boyle, Dunne, Najman et al., in press).

The questionnaire was piloted with a sample of thirty sex workers and then reworked into a final, slightly shorter version. The questions were framed into a readily understandable and acceptable style using language and terminology consistent with that used by workers in the sex industry.

Sampling

Given the covert nature of the sex industry, a number of difficulties existed in relation to obtaining a representative sample of sex workers. These had to do with the following features, which are characteristics of the sex industry:

- The population of sex workers is unknown and, geographically, workers are likely to be widely dispersed.
- Prostitution activities are extremely diverse. They may range, for instance, from a male sex worker using prostitution to survive and a woman working as an escort with a client base comprised of business men. Based on the information available, it was necessary to define prostitution and identify and categorise the range of possible activities.
- The most accessible sex workers are those working in the more 'commercial' aspect of the industry, such as female escort agencies. Generally speaking, those who are most likely to engage in high risk practices, such as injecting drug use or unprotected sex, are probably the most difficult to reach.

The key informant interviews and Advisory Committee provided information which assisted in the identification of the range of types and locations of sex work in Queensland. Based on this information, a desirable quota in each of the identified categories was proposed to ensure a reasonable representation of different groups in the industry. On the basis of the information available, there is reason to believe that the sample achieved is broadly representative of the sex industry as at the time of the study.

Participants were self-referred to the study in response to multiple outreach activities used by the research team to ensure a broad representation of sex workers. These recruitment activities included publicising the study through SQWISI, placing advertisements in the gay newspaper *Queensland Pride* and SQWISI's magazine, *RESPECT*, making direct contact with individuals who placed newspaper and other advertisements for sex-related services, and, finally, word of mouth.

Interviews

A financial gratuity of $20 was offered for completing the semi-structured interview and questionnaire. For most workers this represented an insignificant amount and did not influence their decision to participate in the research. Thus, the payment served as a gesture of appreciation for their time and contribution. For street workers, however, the payment was a likely incentive to participate in the survey.

The objectives of the study were made clear to all participants at the start of the interview. They were given assurances regarding confidentiality and anonymity, and thanked for their participation. In addition, they were informed that the survey was entirely voluntary and that they could choose not to answer particular questions if they so wished.

The sample of sex workers

A total of 230 sex workers were surveyed, including 30 (21 female, 7 male and 2 transsexual workers) who took part in the pilot phase of the study. Table 2.1 shows that the large majority of workers who participated were female. This distribution is believed to be broadly representative of the gender composition of the sex industry at the time, although males and transsexuals may be under-represented.

Table 2.1
Number of respondents by gender

	Number	Per cent
Female	200	87
Male	28	12
Transsexual	2	1
Total	**230**	**100**

Because of the small number of males surveyed, it is difficult to make generalisations about male sex workers or to draw meaningful comparisons between male and female workers. Nonetheless, there is reason to expect that male and female sex workers may differ in many important respects. In view of this, the bulk of this report is concerned with the experience of women in the sex industry, based on the responses of the 200 women who participated in the study.[1] Information pertaining to male sex workers is presented separately as Chapter 11. The transsexual workers are not included in any of the analyses which follow.

At the time of the study, prostitution activities were believed to be occurring in the main Queensland centres. While initial investigations were made in some smaller centres of central and far north Queensland and in a number of remote areas close to mining operations, the study is confined to Brisbane, the Gold and Sunshine Coasts, Townsville and Cairns. Table 2.2 shows the number of interviews conducted in each of these locations.

---

[1] The number of women who responded to a particular item is not always 200 because this total includes the 21 women who participated in the pilot study. Responses to items which were later changed or added to the final version of the interview schedule are therefore available only for the women who completed the final version. Some women also chose not to complete a particular section or series of questions. For this reason, too, the total number of women who responded to a given question may vary.

Table 2.2
Location of interviews

	Number	Per cent
Brisbane	118	51
Cairns	33	14
Townsville	21	9
Sunshine Coast	8	4
Gold Coast	50	22
Total	**230**	**100**

Background characteristics

Many popular myths and stereotypes surround the sex industry and its work force. Yet, our data indicate that female sex workers are a heterogeneous group, with considerable diversity evident with respect to both their current and background circumstances. In terms of most of the socio-demographic variables considered, the sex workers who participated in the study appeared to represent a fairly broad cross-section of the population, with no particular defining characteristics. Perkins (1994) has compared data from four samples of female sex workers derived from studies conducted in Australia between 1985 and 1993. Based on these data, she concluded 'that the social backgrounds of female prostitutes are little different from those of other women' (p.154). Certainly, the following data from our own study would also support this view.

The female workers who took part in the study ranged in age from 16 to 46 years (Figure 2.1). Most, however, were in their 20s or early 30s, and the mean age was 26.5 years. Only 3 per cent were under the age of 18, while 10 per cent were 35 or older. This concentration of women in their 20s to early 30s was also reported by Perkins (1994).

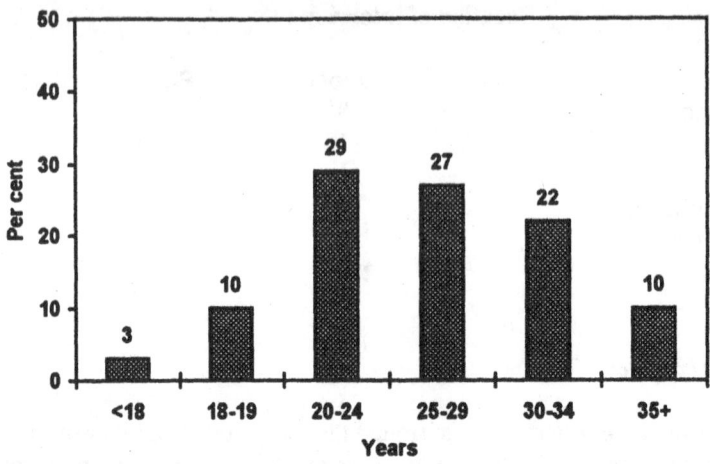

Figure 2.1 Age distribution of 199 female sex workers

Table 2.3 shows that the women most often described themselves as single, having never been married. Even so, it was not unusual for women to be married or living with a partner (26 per cent), a finding which was also reported by Perkins (1994).

Table 2.3
Marital status of 199 female sex workers

	%
Single (never married)	57
Married or living with a partner	26
Divorced or separated	18

Most of the women did not have any children (Table 2.4), but 29 per cent reported having from one to seven children. The children ranged in age from less than 1 to 22 years. In most cases (77 per cent), the child(ren) currently lived with the worker at least some of the time.

Table 2.4
Number of children - 197 female sex workers

	%
None	72
One	15
Two	9
Three or more	5

Table 2.5 shows that the majority of women were Australian born, with small minorities born in New Zealand or the United Kingdom. Most of the women's parents were also born in Australia. Being a highly marginalised group, migrant sex workers, most of whom are likely to be from Asian countries, are not represented in the sample.

Table 2.5
Birthplace of female sex workers and their parents

	Self (N=200) %	Mother (N=199) %	Father (N=199) %
Australia	84	66	60
New Zealand	8	8	8
United Kingdom or Ireland	3	11	11
Europe	3	8	14
Asia	2	1	2
Other	2	7	6

Figure 2.2 provides information about the religious backgrounds of sex workers. Most reported affiliation with a traditional religion while growing up.

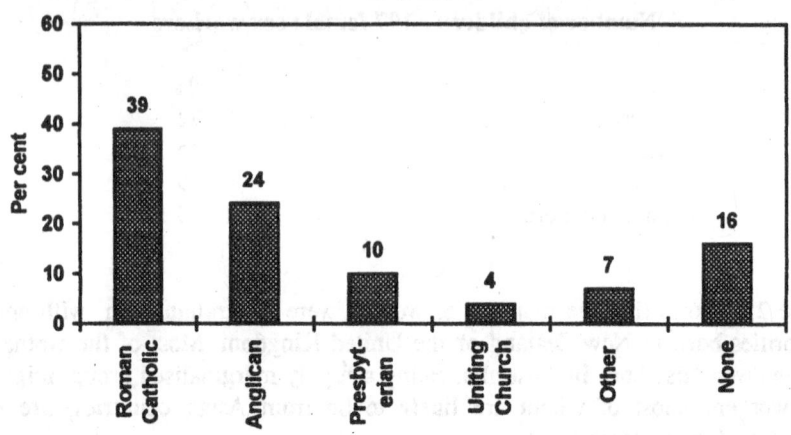

Figure 2.2 Religious affiliation of 198 female sex workers while growing up

In terms of social class, most of the workers self-identified as members of either the working or middle classes (Table 2.6). This reflects a similar pattern to that reported in a survey of self-defined class for the general Australian population (Baxter, Emmison, Western and Western, 1991). Only 8 per cent identified with the middle to upper or upper classes. The four women in the 'other' category described themselves as 'poor' or 'welfare' class.

Table 2.6
Social class (self-defined) of 200 female sex workers

	%
Working class	40
Working to middle class	26
Middle class	25
Middle to upper class	7
Upper class	1
Other	2

At the time of the study, almost 72 per cent of the female sex workers owned, or were paying off, their own car. Home ownership was far less common, with only 19 per cent of women reporting that they owned, or were paying off, a home.

As Table 2.7 shows, the majority of female sex workers did not leave school until the equivalent of year 10 or beyond, with most having left school at age 16 to 17. About 12 per cent left school before the age of 14, including two workers who reported not having been to school at all. At the other extreme, 8 per cent of the women were still studying at age 18 or older.

Table 2.7
Age at which 197 female sex workers left school

	%
14 years or younger	12
15 years	17
16 to 17 years	64
18 years or older	8

The reasons most commonly given by the women for leaving school (Table 2.8) suggested that, in most cases, they had gone as far as they wished at school and had simply decided to leave. While some clearly disliked school, this was not the reason most had left. Very few of the women had been expelled from school or dissuaded from continuing because of poor grades.

Table 2.8
Reasons for leaving school given by 197 female sex workers

	%
Went as far as I wanted	40
Had to find a job	17
Hated school and went as far as I could	16
Went on to further education or good job offer	4
School was irrelevant to me	6
I was kicked out of school	2
Was doing very badly, it wasn't worth staying	1
Other	14

Since leaving school, 24 per cent of the women had begun or completed a course, or some other form of study. The fields of study were varied and included business and secretarial courses, nursing, hairdressing, and university level courses. Overall then, our data are consistent with those of Perkins (1994) who observed that, contrary to much popular belief, female sex workers do not typically come from poverty-stricken backgrounds. Rather, they seem to represent a diversity of socio-economic backgrounds.

Most of the women had left home between the ages of 15 and 17 years (Table 2.9). Relatively few (8 per cent) had left home under the age of 14 and considerably more (37 per cent) had remained at home until they were 18 or older.

Table 2.9
Age at which 197 female sex workers left home

	%
14 years or younger	8
15 to 17 years	55
18 years or older	37

As in the case of school leaving, most women simply seemed to decide that the time had come to leave home (Table 2.10). In some cases, career or relationship choices seemed to be the motivating force behind this decision. Again, relatively few women appeared to have been forced to leave home. Nonetheless, 6 per cent of women had left home as a result of emotional, sexual, or physical abuse while a further 10 per cent clearly had been unhappy at home for other reasons.

Table 2.10
Reason for leaving home given by 197 female sex workers

	%
Just decided it was time	44
Got a job (or went to university/school) and moved away	18
Got married or began a de facto relationship	14
Couldn't stand living at home any longer	10
Emotional, sexual or physical abuse	6
Was kicked out of home	6
Other	3

Some anecdotal reports suggest that sex workers are more likely than other members of the population to have experienced sexual or other forms of abuse during childhood (Seng, 1989). If this is the case, then rates of reported abuse in the present sample are low. During the qualitative interviews, some sex workers, such as the first worker in Inset 2.1, did describe abuse in their own background and linked this abuse directly to their entry to the sex industry. Others noted that they personally knew many sex workers who had experienced sexual abuse as children.

Inset 2.1

> *Were you sexually abused as a child?*
> Yes, I was ... by my mother's de facto.
> *How long did that go on?*
> About five years ... the way I see it I was more or less moulded into the role as prostitute really. I was sort of ... my responses were conditioned.
>
> **(INTERVIEW 4)**
>
> 'I was never sexually abused as a child, I didn't come from a broken family, my mother and father didn't drink, they didn't smoke ... I had a really normal upbringing.'
>
> **(INTERVIEW 15)**

Clearly, however, many other factors are involved in the decision to enter the sex industry as indicated by the second worker in Inset 2.1. Our data, as well as that reported by Perkins (1994), suggest that it would be inaccurate to assume that all or most sex workers had grown up in abusive family settings.

Summary

This chapter has described the background, methods and respondent characteristics of a survey of 230 Queensland sex workers. Most (87 per cent) of those who participated were female workers operating in Brisbane and the Gold Coast. The women ranged in age from 16 to 46 years and the large majority were Australian-born. While many stereotypes are held about sex workers, the socio-demographic profile of the workers surveyed in this study indicated that sex workers are a heterogeneous group. The wide diversity of backgrounds indicates that there is unlikely to be any single factor predisposing women to enter the sex industry. This level of diversity is highlighted throughout the remaining chapters which aim to present a detailed picture of various aspects of the sex industry in Queensland.

3   The experience of sex work

Workers in the sex industry are involved in an extremely diverse range of work situations. Many workers may also be involved in more than one type of work or move in and out of work situations quite regularly. As already noted, social and political factors also contribute to the character and changing nature of the industry. While these features of the industry make it difficult to categorise sex workers according to the type of work performed, there is reason to expect that practices and attitudes may vary depending on the work setting from which a worker operates.

Range of work settings

The qualitative data and key informant interviews indicated that sex workers tended to locate their activities in one of five settings as listed and described in Inset 3.1. These settings tend to differ across a range of characteristics including where the sex work is performed, the type of client attracted, the level of physical risk involved, and the income-earning potential.

Inset 3.1

Massage parlour or brothel
These establishments are managed premises often with a receptionist. Clients arrive and may ask for a regular worker or may be given a choice from the workers available. Workers are provided with a percentage of the money they earn, sometimes being allowed to keep all the money for 'extras' they provide. Shifts of six to eight hours are common although some workers may work longer shifts on occasions.

Parlour escort business
Similar to massage parlours or brothels, these establishments may offer sex on the premises from a number of available women. Alternatively, a client can request an outcall at a venue of their choice usually at the client's home, or a motel or hotel room. This type of establishment may provide for a wide range of client preferences, and numbers appeared to be growing around the time this survey was conducted.

Escort agency
These agencies almost exclusively do outcalls. Often the sex worker may have a mobile phone or may make arrangements to receive phone calls at an agency. If an agency is involved it usually retains a fee. In addition, there is a driver who takes the worker to the site and who provides a level of protection. Drivers sometimes wait to make certain that the worker is safe before leaving.

Street workers
This type of worker appeared to be relatively uncommon in Queensland at the time of the survey. However, because they are difficult to locate, they may be under-represented in this study. Street workers may use hotels as a base for locating clients. Generally, the working conditions for street workers are poor. They have little protection and may have little contact with the organised sex industry.

Private workers
Private workers are usually in business on their own, or occasionally with another worker. They need to build up a clientele and/or personally advertise their services to provide them with sufficient work. They may do outcalls as well as incalls and some, usually more experienced workers, may opt to rent or purchase a house from which to operate. With a regular clientele, issues of personal safety may become a lower priority. Overall, these self-employed workers might be expected to be more resourceful than their counterparts in some other work settings.

Current work locations

The women who took part in the study were asked which of the above categories they thought best described their work situation. Usually, this was also the type of work which provided the highest percentage of their income derived from the sex industry. Table 3.1 shows the distribution of workers across the various categories.

Table 3.1
Current work location of 200 female sex workers

	%
Massage parlour or brothel	16
Parlour escort	24
Escort agency	28
Street	6
Private	26

Similar numbers of women were employed in private and escort work (both parlour- and agency-based) and, together, these three categories of work accounted for about 80 per cent of the sample. Fewer women worked in massage parlours or brothels, and street work was relatively rare.

Initial work locations

Table 3.2 examines where the workers began in the industry. Massage parlours, brothels and escort agencies were the point of entry to the sex industry for more than three quarters of the women. Only 12 per cent had begun working from the street and it was even less common for workers to have begun working from a private setting.

Table 3.2
Work location in which 200 female sex workers started in the sex industry

	%
Massage parlour or brothel	41
Escort agency	37
Private	7
Street	12
Other	4

These data were collected shortly after the Fitzgerald Inquiry had led to the closure of many brothels from which many of the women interviewed presumably had begun working. It would appear likely that if the research were to be repeated now, a different set of responses would be obtained given that large brothels have been made illegal, and virtually none are operating. Also, both clients and workers are now liable to legal sanctions.

A comparison of the data in Tables 3.1 and 3.2 gives some perspective on the changing nature of sex work and how workers may begin in one type of work but, over time, move to another. Many women who had started in, say, a massage parlour had moved into private work. Similarly, some women who had started on the street had subsequently moved into one of the other categories of work.

It was also apparent that many women had worked in a variety of settings since entering the sex industry (Figure 3.1). The majority had at some time worked for an escort agency, or massage parlour. By contrast, few had ever worked from a street or a hotel.

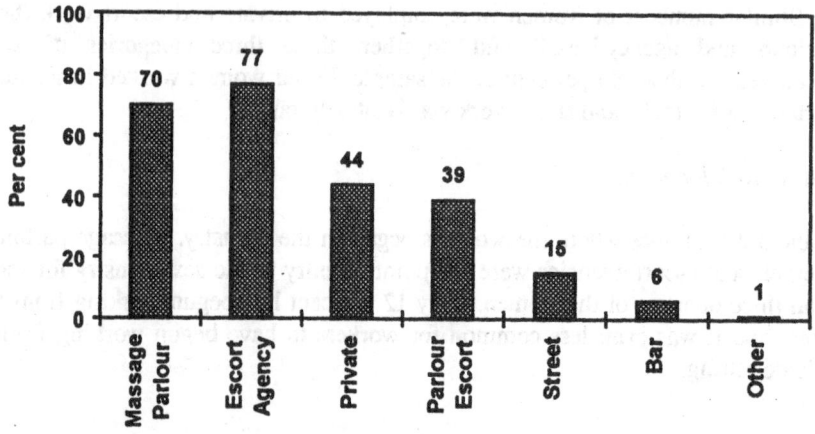

Figure 3.1   Types of work performed by 200 female sex workers since starting in the industry (multiple responses possible)

Sex workers have clear preferences about the types of work setting from which they offer their services. This is demonstrated in Table 3.3 which shows how the women ranked the various categories of sex work. Very few women would choose to do street or hotel work if other options were available. Parlour, escort and private are clearly the most popular types of sex work. Such preferences appear to reflect concerns with personal safety, income earning potential and the opportunity to have a more extended relationship with a client.

Table 3.3
Ratings of work settings by 200 female sex workers

	Rate 1 %	Rate 2 %	Rate 3 %	Rate 4 %
Massage parlour or brothel	33	28	24	15
Escort agency	27	46	18	9
Private work	35	13	35	17
Street work	0	1	2	97
Bar or hotel work	0	0	5	95

Further understanding of the reasons for these preferences can be derived from the qualitative data presented in Insets 3.2 and 3.3. Inset 3.2 provides one view of work from an escort service. Here the worker is concerned by the lack of safety involved in making outcalls. The second worker in Inset 3.2 notes that parlour work is easier, one just has to turn up and everything else is provided. Here there seems to be a distinction between workers who simply provide a sex service, but in a very controlled environment, and those who are apparently willing to work in a variety of arrangements because they find the latter more financially rewarding or interesting.

Inset 3.2

> 'I've done a little bit of escort work, but didn't like it. You can't relax, you're in someone else's private home, you don't know who is there other than yourself and the client. I much prefer the parlour because you've got more protection and other girls around you. It's a much safer environment.'
> **(INTERVIEW 10)**
> 'Parlour work ... it's more controlled, I don't have to worry about advertising or walking around the streets, I don't have to worry about setting up a place of my own. I don't have to worry about clients getting heavy. The parlour owner does all the advertising, all I have to do is turn up and be there.'
> **(INTERVIEW 13)**

However, such preferences were by no means universal. In Inset 3.3 the first worker expresses a willingness to do escort work but makes it clear that she had a driver who would be on a two-way radio and who maintained surveillance until it was clear that she was safe. Like the other workers in Inset 3.3, she also alludes to the trade-off that exists in terms of the greater protection offered by parlours and the greater earning potential of private work. They refer specifically to the shift to private work necessitated for many workers by changes to the sex industry which were introduced during the course of the study.

Inset 3.3

> 'I didn't mind the private homes, I felt safe. But I had a good boss, a good driver. They always handled the money ... they came to the door with you ... they were on two-way in the car ... if you didn't ring in within five minutes ... the driver would be back to see what's going on. I think street work is the pits ... the risks are just too great ... the parlour work ... it was safe ... in escorts you got a different type of client ... they always tipped.'
> **(INTERVIEW 14)**
>
> 'Before the Inquiry there were lots of agencies run by what they used to call syndicates, and the girls I felt were exploited through those agencies, but they had the safety of working in places like that ... even though they were exploited financially and in other ways, like being expected to do things they didn't want to do with clients just to keep their jobs.'
> **(INTERVIEW 1)**
>
> 'At least [private workers] don't have to part with half their money or at times even more than half ... but it's more dangerous to work. Before in the parlour industry, at least even though you were working for stand-over merchants, if something happened, the people were right there, but now there's no one ...'
> **(INTERVIEW 11)**

Length of time in the sex industry

Table 3.4 shows the length of time the women had worked in the sex industry. The variation is considerable, with 33 per cent having been in the industry for less than two years and some 15 per cent having been in the industry for ten years or more. The data suggest that the women differ widely in their level of work experience, with a substantial proportion being fairly recent recruits and another group being long-term workers.

Table 3.4
Length of time 198 female workers had worked in the sex industry

	%
Less than 2 years	33
2 to 9 years	52
10 or more years	15

The women had worked in Queensland for varying periods of time, ranging from one week to 20 years, but usually for one year or longer (Figure 3.2). About one quarter of the sample had worked in the Queensland sex industry for less than one year.

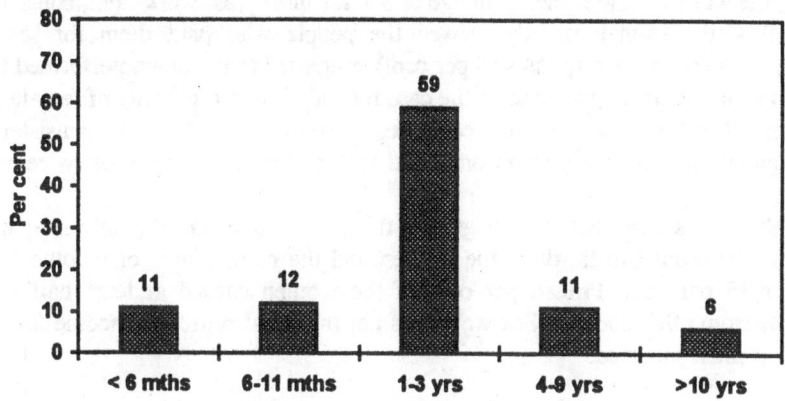

Figure 3.2 Length of time 176 sex workers had worked in Queensland

Many women (51 per cent) had also worked in Australian states other than Queensland and a small number (4 per cent) had worked overseas (Table 3.5). These data further illustrate the diversity of work experience characteristic of the sex workers who took part in the study.

Table 3.5
Other work locations of 178 female sex workers
(multiple responses possible)

	%
Queensland only	49
New South Wales	39
Victoria	22
South Australia	4
Western Australia	4
ACT	4
Northern Territory	2
Tasmania	1
Overseas	4

Sex work as work

Almost all the female workers who took part in the study exchanged sex exclusively for money (97 per cent). Very few received payment of any other kind, such as in the form of commodities, drugs or services. Almost always (94 per cent), the women viewed the exchange of sex for money as 'work' and, consistent with this, the women usually viewed the people who paid them for sex as 'clients'. While some responses (8 per cent) suggested that women performed this work to survive, this appears to be the case for only a small minority of female sex workers. Most women (66 per cent) reported that they worked consistently throughout the year. Only about one third took a short break once or twice each year.

Table 3.6 shows that money gained from sex work was the sole source of income for about two thirds of the women and the main source of income for a further 18 per cent. Fifteen per cent of the women earned at least half their income from other sources. Sex work was not the usual source of income for two of the women surveyed.

Table 3.6
Proportion of income derived from sex work by 199 female sex workers

	%
All	67
Most	18
About half	9
Some	6
None	1

Entering the sex industry

Two key issues of both legal and social interest are the age at which workers enter the sex industry and the sequence of events and combination of factors which lead them to enter the industry. Our qualitative interviews indicated that there was not always a clear demarcation between formal entry to the 'paid' sex industry and informal sexual activity in which payment may be in kind for the services provided.

This is well illustrated by the first worker in Inset 3.4 who stated that she entered the industry at the age of 16, but had been living on the streets since the age of 12 and had engaged in sexual activity prior to considering herself a worker. Indeed she defined herself as a worker only when she began working in a parlour. Prior to that she was a non-professional worker who may have exchanged sex for accommodation, food and the like.

Inset 3.4

> *At what age did you start in the sex industry?*
> Well it depends what you call ... for me I considered when I first walked into a parlour working properly but I started doing hand jobs and things like that ... I had never had sex with anyone so I never considered myself to be a sex worker until I was sixteen, but I probably started when I was about twelve, when I was living on the streets ...
> *So what led up to your starting in the industry?*
> Nowhere to live, no money and an offer came along and it just seemed alright at the time too, and drugs ... I was into drugs too so I had to get money for drugs.
> *How did you end up on the street at twelve?*
> I ran away from home. I was in a home and I just ran away. I'd just had enough.
> **(INTERVIEW 12)**
>
> 'It was about five years ago [at age 22] that I started. I tried working straight jobs, but because I was a senior they were preferring juniors...'
> **(INTERVIEW 10)**

The second worker in Inset 3.4 entered the sex industry under very different circumstances. She had worked at other jobs but entered the industry at the age of 22 when she had difficulty getting another job because of her age.

The diversity of entry to the sex industry is further emphasised by the workers whose responses appear in Inset 3.5. While some would perhaps stereotype the industry as having many negative features, some respondents report they have found it to have many attractions. Some workers pointed out that they enjoyed the company of other people in the industry.

Inset 3.5

> 'I was 26. I just looked it up in the paper ... I liked it ... I liked the people... I like the money ... I enjoy the company of the people I work with ...'
> **(INTERVIEW 14)**
>
> 'I just find it so much more gratifying than being stuck in a factory ... it's just a lot more dynamic ... like the meeting people, you're making friends and you're just living life a lot more ...'
> **(INTERVIEW 4)**
>
> 'I've been working for 18 months now and I started when I was 32. I was like a duck to water and wished to hell that I got into it years ago.'
> **(INTERVIEW 21)**

Inset 3.6, however, provides a clear contrast to the above respondents. The first respondent explains that her mother, who owned a brothel at the time, arranged for her then teenage daughter to service two clients on the basis that sex was not a commodity to be given away. Also described is the history of a young woman who was 14 when she began sex work. She reports that she had only had sex on one occasion before beginning as a sex worker and she was clearly confused at the time about the services she was expected to provide.

Inset 3.6

> 'See I never made a conscious decision to professionally start work. I was probably about 15 or I might have been 16 when my mother actually lined up a couple of clients for me ... her attitude was ... you're having sex anyway ... you may as well get paid for it ... it was a horrible experience at the time.'
>
> **(INTERVIEW 16)**
>
> 'I started in the industry when I was around 14 and I was actually in an unemployment office and as I walked out of this unemployment office this man asked me if I was interested in modelling ... he gave me the address so I rocked around there ... asked her about modelling and she said "No, we need masseurs", so I said "What's that?" and she explained a little about it. My first job was full French* and I didn't know what that was. I came out of the room with all this money and I said ... "He wanted full French and he gave me all this money" and I said "I don't know what it is!" and she told me and I was sick ... I went and did the job and I found it a little easier each time. I'd only had sex once before I started working.'
>
> * Oral sex performed on the client to ejaculation.
>
> **(INTERVIEW 18)**

Age at entry to the sex industry

Figure 3.3 shows that most female workers (65 per cent) entered the industry in their later teens or early 20s. A very small minority (4 per cent) had begun working in the sex industry before age 15. At the other extreme, 14 per cent of workers entered the industry at age 30 or older. The mean age at entry into the sex industry was 21.3 years. These patterns are highly consistent with data reported by Perkins (1994) and derived from other Australian samples of female sex workers. The age at which workers enter the industry has significance for both their health and their legal position. Workers who enter the industry in their early teens may be exposed to a variety of additional risks. There is also the possibility that workers who enter the industry in the older age groups differ from others in a number of important respects, for example, in the sex services they provide, the clients they attract and their consequent exposure to the risk of HIV/AIDS.

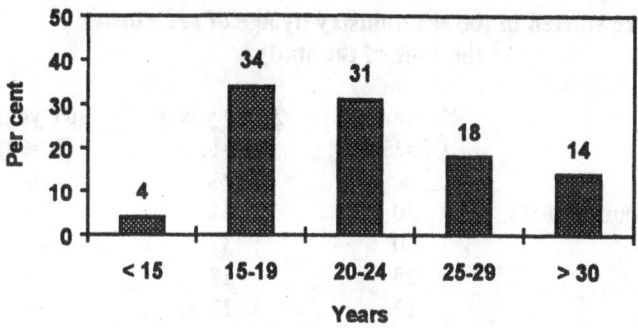

Figure 3.3 Age at which 199 female workers started in the sex industry

Table 3.7 provides a breakdown of the age at which workers entered the sex industry according to their age at the time of the interview and the length of time they had worked in the industry. As would be expected, these variables are closely related. Older workers had been in the industry longer than young workers and those who had spent most time in the industry had started at a younger age.

Table 3.7
Current age of sex workers by age entered and length of time in industry

Current age	Age entered			Years in industry		
	<20	20-29	30+	<2	2-9	10+
Less than 20 years						
(N=25) %	100	--	--	64	36	--
20 to 29 years						
(N=111) %	38	62	--	32	55	13
30 years and older						
(N=63) %	11	46	43	17	57	25

Marked age differences were evident in relation to where workers had started in the industry (Table 3.8). The large majority of older workers had begun work in massage parlours and escort agencies, while younger workers were more likely to have commenced work in escort agencies or on the street.

Table 3.8
Where started in the sex industry by age of sex worker at the time of the study

	<20 years (N=25) %	20-29 years (N=111) %	30+ years (N=63) %
Massage parlour/brothel	20	42	48
Escort agency	40	32	43
Street	28	13	5
Other	12	13	5

As the younger workers are most likely to have entered the industry since the Fitzgerald Inquiry, this gives an indication of a likely trend in current recruitment into the sex industry. Undoubtedly, street work entails greater dangers to the health and safety of sex workers and a trend to more work of this type would appear to be highly undesirable.

Table 3.9 considers each of the categories of work in terms of the number of workers who were young, had been in the industry for a lengthy period, and who had started at a young age. The most striking difference involves the small group of street workers. While they are significantly younger ($p = 0.05$), as a group they have nonetheless been working longer than the other workers ($p < 0.001$). Consistent with this, they are also more likely to have entered the industry at a younger age ($p < 0.01$). Private workers also tended to have been working for longer periods but, unlike street workers, also tended to be older at the time of the interview.

Table 3.9
Type of work location by selected worker characteristics

Worker characteristic	Brothel (N=31) %	Parlour Escort (N=48) %	Escort Agency (N=55) %	Street (N=11) %	Private (N=53) %
Aged < 20 yrs	19	13	16	27	2
Worked 10+ years	10	4	9	45	28
< 20 yrs when started	45	35	29	91	32

Street workers also differed quite markedly from other workers in relation to certain other socio-demographic characteristics. For example, some 70 per cent had left school at 14 or younger compared with 5 to 16 per cent in the other work categories. Similarly, 60 per cent of the street workers had left home at 14 or younger compared with no more than 7 per cent of other workers. In both cases this difference is statistically significant beyond the 0.001 level.

Reasons for entering the sex industry

Both the qualitative and quantitative data revealed that in the majority of cases, the decision to enter the sex industry appeared to be motivated by financial considerations together with a perceived lack of other employment options. Based on the survey data, Table 3.10 provides the reasons workers gave for entering the industry. Needing money was the reason most frequently nominated (71 per cent) followed by being unable to get another job (20 per cent). For a small proportion of women (15 per cent) sex work offered the opportunity to save for a particular material goal.

Table 3.10
Main reason for entering the sex industry – 200 female sex workers
(multiple responses possible)

	%
I just needed the money	71
I couldn't get another job	20
I had a particular goal in mind (e.g., house, car)	15
Purely for survival	10
It was good money and flexible hours	8
I just sort of drifted into it	5
Needed money to pay for drugs	3

If these responses are considered in terms of intrinsic and extrinsic work satisfaction, one gains the impression that workers enter this industry for purely extrinsic reasons, the most important of which involves the financial reimbursement. Data reported by Perkins (1994) also indicated that women's reasons for entering the sex industry are usually closely related to economic consideration.

Employment before entering the sex industry

Table 3.11 examines the employment situation of workers before they entered the sex industry. Two types of employment history seem common. Almost half the workers were not employed prior to entering the industry while one third were employed full time in some other capacity. The relatively large number of women who came from a background of unemployment again highlights financial issues as being a primary consideration of many workers who entered the industry.

Table 3.11
Employment of 200 female sex workers prior to entering the sex industry

	%
Not employed	46
Full-time employed	34
Part-time employed	8
Home duties	7
Student	4
Casual employment	3

Living arrangements before entering the sex industry

Just under half the women (41 per cent) were living with friends in shared accommodation before they entered the sex industry, but other living arrangements were not uncommon (Table 3.12). Some 20 per cent of women were living with a partner, while 13 per cent were living with their parents or other relatives. In this sample of sex workers, relatively few had begun work while living on the street.

Table 3.12
Living arrangements of 199 female sex workers when they entered the sex industry

	%
Sharing with friends	41
Living alone	21
Living with parents/relatives	13
Living with a partner who had a job	11
Living with a partner who was unemployed	10
Living on the street	5

The majority of women had no dependants when they joined the sex industry but a small number were responsible for the financial support of up to five people (Table 3.13). In relatively few cases then are financial burdens associated with supporting others likely to have motivated women to enter the sex industry. Nonetheless, as shown shortly, for some women sex work offered a source of income enabling them to provide a standard of living for their children which otherwise may not have been possible.

Table 3.13
Number of dependants at time of entry to sex industry – 198 female sex workers

	%
None	83
One	9
Two	5
Three or more	3

Leaving and re-entering the industry

Table 3.14 shows that about one third of women had, on at least one occasion, left the sex industry for at least six months.

Table 3.14
Number of times 195 female sex workers had left the industry for more than six months

	%
Never	69
Once	22
Twice	6
Three times or more	2

They had left for a variety of reasons, as shown in Table 3.15. There is no single reason which seems to motivate workers to leave, but one gains the impression that many women simply tire of the industry and the clients. Another reason for leaving concerns the woman's relationship with her partner. In a relatively small number of cases, it appeared to be an enforced absence from the industry due for example, to pregnancy, health problems, imprisonment, or an unworkable relationship with police. Financial considerations, which are the main reasons for entering the industry in the first place, were also the single most common reason for returning to the industry following a temporary absence. Presumably, some women may have left the industry with the intention of returning at a later time. Others may have intended to leave the industry permanently only to re-enter for financial reasons.

Table 3.15
Reasons for leaving sex industry – 60 women who had left for at least six months (multiple responses possible)

	%
Just had enough	40
Sick of the clients	22
My partner wanted me to/got married	20
Fell pregnant	13
Found a good job/further education	2
Went on holiday	2
I obtained my goal	5
Was concerned about AIDS or other STDs	5
Other health problems	2
Was in jail	3
Police forced me out	5
Other	8

The qualitative interviews strongly reinforced the notion that many workers reach a point where they feel they need to leave the sex industry, at least temporarily. Yet, as the third worker in Inset 3.7 indicates, it may be difficult for some workers to leave permanently because they have become accustomed to a certain standard of living that they could not otherwise maintain.

Inset 3.7

> 'I worked intermittently, I found I couldn't cope emotionally, mentally with the business for long periods of time, so I would stick at it for a time then go back to a straight job.'
>
> **(INTERVIEW 1)**
>
> 'It is a profession, but I can't see myself just keeping going with it; you have to have a break in it somewhere along the line, just pull yourself out of it, because of the pressure ... the stress and the strain and you need to give your body a rest, which is really important ...'
>
> **(INTERVIEW 10)**
>
> 'Once you get used to living on a high income, you know, when you've got all this money coming in, it's very hard to stop yourself and go back to a normal ... whatever that might be ... wage and a normal sort of standard of living. I mean, I realise that I probably lost touch with reality on what an actual normal standard of living is.'
>
> **(INTERVIEW 5)**

Desire to leave the industry

Just less than one third of the female workers (29 per cent) stated that they wanted to leave the sex industry at the time of the study interview. Women who were currently working on the street were more likely to want to leave the industry: 73 per cent compared with 18 to 34 per cent in the other work categories ($p < 0.01$).

Inset 3.8 provides one example of a worker who planned to leave soon after the interview was conducted. She planned to marry and have children and felt certain that she would not return to the industry.

Inset 3.8

Why are you leaving work?
It's time in my life where I need to settle more. I have worked five years and I don't want to keep going. I want to go home, turn into a mother and a housewife, I suppose.
Do you think you would come back to the industry at any time?
No, I don't think so. Not once I have settled, got married and had children.
(INTERVIEW 10)

The decision to continue working in the industry despite a desire to leave was once again usually motivated by financial considerations. Of those who wanted to leave the industry, most (72 per cent) stated that they did not leave because they simply needed the money too much and 4 per cent indicated they were still working towards a pre-set goal. Clearly, however, a perception that alternative employment options are limited also contributed to the decision to stay in the industry for many workers (32 per cent). This confirms that the extrinsic rewards associated with being in the industry are sufficient to encourage the majority to remain in their current work role. Even though one third of workers express the view that they would like to leave, financial considerations seem to be sufficient to retain the workers, at least temporarily.

Sex workers' social networks

Of interest is the question of whether the family and friends of sex workers are aware of their work, or whether workers tend to create a clear division between their work and personal lives. Related to this is the possibility that sex workers are a relatively insular group, with the majority of their social contact confined to other workers in the industry.

Family and friends

For most workers, there was some level of secrecy about their involvement in the sex industry. Table 3.16 shows that it was uncommon for all, or even most, of the sex workers' family members or close friends to be aware of their work. More than two thirds of the women reported that none of their family members were aware of their involvement in the sex industry. However, most had at least some close friends or acquaintances who knew that they were sex workers.

Table 3.16
Others' awareness of 198 female sex workers' involvement in the industry

	Family members %	Close friends %	Acquaintances %	Neighbours %
None	69	15	47	90
Some	19	54	42	7
Most	2	15	6	1
All	11	17	5	3

Other workers in the sex industry

As shown in Table 3.17, all the women knew at least one other female sex worker in the geographical area in which they worked and the majority (64 per cent) claimed to know at least 10 other workers. By contrast, the women as a group knew of few male, and even fewer transsexual, workers. Perkins (1994) found that many sex workers who worked alone made themselves known to each other for reasons of security and company and even the sharing of clients.

Table 3.17
Number of other workers (in same city or town) known to 200 female sex workers

	Females %	Males %	Transsexuals %
None	0	67	87
1 to 4	13	24	11
5 to 9	24	5	1
10 to 19	29	4	1
20 or more	35	1	1

Table 3.18 suggests that the workers did not confine their social contacts to the sex industry with friends both within and outside the industry. Relatively few stated that all four of their closest friends were either other workers or from outside the industry. It appears from these data that sex workers rarely form close friendships with clients.

Table 3.18
Thinking about your closest friends, how many of them are:

	Other workers* %	Clients* %	Private partner* %	People outside the industry* %
None	35	99	82	23
One	27	1	18	9
Two	14	0	0	19
Three	8	0	0	25
Four	16	0	0	24

* N ranges from 185 to 200

Inset 3.9 provides a qualitative perspective on the issue of sex workers 'coming out' to family and friends. While some sex workers elect to tell family and friends about their work and simply accept the consequences, others appear to lead something of a 'double life', living with a fear of being alienated from family and friends.

Inset 3.9

> 'I had my two sets of friends. The friends that knew that I worked and the friends who didn't know I worked. I always had the feeling that with the people I didn't tell that if I had told them, I would have been personally rejected by them.'
>
> (INTERVIEW 1)
>
> 'My mother screamed ... I was 14 when I told her ... my father said "You're very rebellious and if I tell you not to do this I know you're going to go ahead and do it so what I'm going to tell you stands from now till the day you die ... the door's always open and if you're in trouble you come home"... so my parents didn't like it but you know they've learned to accept it ... A couple of my friends find it fascinating ... a couple of people that I've met heard I was a worker but didn't know me ... they were worried about their husbands ... Most people are just curious about it.'
>
> (INTERVIEW 18)
>
> 'I'm petrified of my mum and dad finding out, or my brother.'
>
> (INTERVIEW 21)

Summary

The sequence of factors which lead people to choose particular types of work are not well understood. Extrinsic factors such as the pay, conditions and hours of work, as well as intrinsic factors such as the satisfaction and sense of achievement associated with the work, can all influence work choices. Women in this study entered the sex industry in differing ways but most often because the opportunity presented at a time of financial need. A limited range of alternative employment options, particularly those which provide comparable levels of income, was also a factor: 20 per cent indicated that they had not been able to find any other form of employment and almost half the women were unemployed before entering the industry. Most of the women had entered the industry in their later teens or early twenties and very few had begun working in the sex industry before the age of 15.

While about one third of workers expressed dissatisfaction with the work itself in that they wished to leave the industry at the time of the study, the extrinsic rewards and the lack of ready employment alternatives seemed to deter them from leaving. Financial incentives are also the main reason for resuming sex work among workers who had previously decided to leave.

Within the sex industry itself there is considerable diversity in terms of the range of work settings and level of work experience. The majority of women were first employed in massage parlours or escort agencies, with younger women more likely to have started work in escort agencies or on the street. Two thirds of the workers were currently operating from organised settings while about one quarter operated from private settings. Street work was viewed as a highly unattractive option by workers themselves and only 6 per cent of the women surveyed were working on the street at the time of the study.

4 Knowledge and attitudes about safe sex practices

This chapter provides an overview of the level of awareness among female sex workers of HIV/AIDS and a variety of risk factors that may be associated with its transmission. We begin by examining the degree to which workers see themselves at risk of becoming infected with HIV and the level of anxiety associated with this possibility. We then explore the attitudinal and informational context in which sex workers were operating at the time of the study by examining why workers considered themselves to be at high (or low) risk, their attitudes regarding the level of risk associated with a range of specific behaviours and their level of basic knowledge about HIV/AIDS. During the interviews HIV was referred to as 'the AIDS virus' because this was found to be the term best understood by the sex workers in the pilot phase of the study.

Perceived risk of contracting HIV/AIDS

Most workers (84 per cent) believed that their risk of becoming infected with the AIDS virus was small or non-existent (Figure 4.1). Nonetheless, some 16 per cent of workers thought they had at least a chance of contracting the virus. None of the workers interviewed reported already being infected.

The degree to which workers perceived themselves at risk of HIV infection was significantly associated with type of work ($p < 0.001$). As shown in Table 4.1, most of the small group of street workers considered their risk to be high or reasonably high, compared with only a minority of women in the other work categories. Other worker characteristics (present age, age started in the industry, and length of time in the industry) were not associated with personal perceptions of HIV/AIDS-related risk.

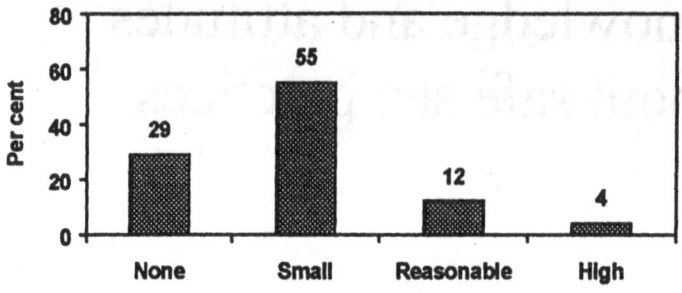

Figure 4.1 Chance of contracting HIV/AIDS as perceived by 197 female sex workers

Table 4.1
Perceived chance of contracting HIV/AIDS by type of work

	Brothel (N=31)	Parlour Escort (N=47)	Escort Agency (N=56)	Street (N=10)	Private (N=53)
	%	%	%	%	%
None	19	23	38	20	32
Small	71	62	48	0	58
Reasonable/high	10	15	14	80	9

About one third of the female sex workers (34 per cent) reported moderate or high levels of anxiety in relation to HIV/AIDS while one fifth stated that they were not worried at all (Table 4.2).

Table 4.2
Level of anxiety about contracting HIV/AIDS among 197 female sex workers

	%
Not worried at all	21
Slightly anxious	45
Moderately anxious	20
Very anxious	14

The age at which workers entered the sex industry was significantly associated with level of HIV/AIDS-related anxiety ($p = 0.002$) but within each of the three age groups, there was considerable variation. Table 4.3 shows that the group of women who entered the sex industry at a younger age was characterised by higher rates of both no anxiety and high anxiety about HIV/AIDS when compared with women in the older age groups. This was accompanied by a (non-significant) trend towards higher levels of anxiety among workers who were younger at the time of the study: 48 per cent of those aged under 20, compared with 28 per cent of those aged 30 or older, were very or moderately anxious about HIV/AIDS. The length of time a worker had been in the industry was not associated with level of anxiety.

Table 4.3
Level of anxiety about contracting HIV/AIDS by age worker entered the sex industry

	<20 (N=74) %	20-29 (N=95) %	30+ (N=27) %
Not anxious at all	31	11	26
Slightly anxious	28	56	52
Moderately or very anxious	41	33	22

Table 4.4 shows that, depending on their type of work, female sex workers may also differ in terms of HIV/AIDS-related anxiety (p = 0.05). There was a tendency for street workers to express the most (and private workers the least) anxiety about HIV/AIDS.

Table 4.4
Level of anxiety about contracting HIV/AIDS by type of work

	Brothel (N=31) %	Parlour Escort (N=48) %	Escort Agency (N=56) %	Street (N=10) %	Private (N=52) %
Not anxious at all	26	15	16	10	31
Slightly anxious	45	35	52	30	48
Moderately or very anxious	29	50	32	60	21

· The comments of the workers in Inset 4.1 illustrate two themes which frequently emerged in relation to the risk of HIV/AIDS during the qualitative interviews. Many workers acknowledged that exposure to the risk of HIV/AIDS was inherent in their work and that, by taking precautions, risks could be minimised but not eliminated altogether. At the same time, some workers, such as the third worker in Inset 4.1, pointed out that their risk was probably no greater than that of other members of the population who engage in casual sexual encounters and who may take fewer precautions.

Inset 4.1

> *Do you think you are more at risk working in the industry than other people?*
> Of course, I think you are, because you are having more sex partners than if you had one person in your private life and when you're having sex with one person, you can both go and be checked every three months and both prove to each other on paper that you're okay. You can't do that to every client that walks in the door. If he says he's okay and he wears a condom, if the condom breaks you are going to be worried. You might see between four and ten clients a day, so because of the number of clients you see the chances of a condom breaking is higher.
>
> **(INTERVIEW 1)**
>
> *How worried are you about HIV?*
> It's not something that I greatly worry about myself, it's the good old 'it'll never happen to me' sort of line, but I try ... I don't dwell on it, I don't sort of ... my every second thought isn't on it, it'll cross my mind every now and then, but I try and keep myself as safe as possible. I don't use needles and I use condoms all the time, and you know, making sure that they're put on properly, minimising your risk ... you can minimise your risks.
>
> *Do you think you're more at risk than someone who doesn't work in the industry?*
> I don't know, I mean, you go out to nightclubs and you see these girls and guys you know, looking to pick up a member of the opposite sex, now I don't know how meticulous they are in watching their own health. I do believe that you've got more chance of getting something, catching something from someone from a nightclub than you do off a worker ...
>
> **(INTERVIEW 5)**

Most sex workers are likely to be exposed to at least some particularly high risk situations and the encounter described in Inset 4.2 is one such example. In this instance, a client disclosed to the sex worker that he was HIV positive. While no sexual activity took place with the worker, the incident highlights how a lack of awareness about health issues combined with exposure to potentially high risk situations may leave some sex workers extremely vulnerable.

Inset 4.2

And do you think workers in the sex industry are at any special risk?
Yes, they are. Yes. Even recently I know of a girl that was sent out from another owner to an AIDS patient and all he really wanted was someone to talk to, and that girl tried to coax him into bed. I mean, she was a new girl, ignorant, totally ignorant, and luckily for her the guy was a decent, really decent, nice guy and he really only wanted her there to talk to him. He didn't want sex, he was HIV positive, he was having trouble dealing with it.
(INTERVIEW 11)

Reasons for variations in perceived risk of HIV/AIDS

For a variety of reasons, a worker's (subjective) perception of risk may differ from her actual (objective) level of risk. From a health point of view, it is important to know whether high levels of concern expressed by some workers about HIV/AIDS reflected greater exposure to known HIV risk factors or heightened sensitivity and awareness about the disease. A perception of low risk, or a lower level of anxiety, could be due to greater awareness of risks together with more cautious behaviours. On the other hand, a perception of low risk might simply reflect a lack of awareness about the level of risk. This issue is explored further in Tables 4.5 and 4.6, which summarise women's responses to the question of why they believed they were (or were not) at risk for HIV infection.

Table 4.5
Reasons given by 166 female sex workers for small or no chance of HIV/AIDS infection (multiple responses possible)

	%
I always use condoms	95
I don't inject drugs	60
I check my clients	57
I go for regular STD checks	57
My clients are unlikely to be infected	11
I do not see homosexual men or IV drug users	11
I pick my clients carefully	11
My private partner is AIDS free	9
I only have sex without condoms with my regular partner	8
My regular partner does not engage in anything risky	7
I inject drugs but I don't share needles and syringes	5
I always clean my needle and syringe if I share	1

Overwhelmingly, the women who thought their chance of contracting AIDS was small or nonexistent believed this was so because they always used condoms (Table 4.5). In addition, many women also stated that their risk was low because they did not use injecting drugs. Ineffective methods of HIV/AIDS prevention, including checking clients and having regular STD checks, were cited by a sizeable number of the workers but the data suggest that these were considered as adjuncts to condom use rather than preventive measures of themselves.

The small group of women who believed they were at reasonable or greater level of risk of infection were asked why they thought this was so. Their answers indicated that they were exposed to potentially high-risk situations (Table 4.6). Highlighted was the fact that, even when condoms are used, breakages can and do occur. Yet, only a relatively small proportion of the sex workers who took part in the study indicated that this placed them at substantial risk of HIV infection. Presumably, some women in the group who viewed their HIV/AIDS risk as low would have experienced, or would at least be aware of, the potential for condom breakages. Again, there was also a suggestion that some workers believed regular medical checks contributed to a reduction in HIV/AIDS risk.

Table 4.6
Reasons given by 29 female sex workers for reasonable or greater chance of HIV/AIDS infection (multiple responses possible)

	%
Condoms sometimes break	48
I don't always use condoms	21
My clients are likely to be infected	17
I don't go for regular check-ups	14
I inject drugs and share needles	3
My partner is HIV positive	0
I see homosexual men injecting drug users	0

It was noted in Table 4.4 that type of work was significantly associated with the perception of risk for HIV/AIDS and that street workers considered themselves to be particularly vulnerable. The reasons why street workers held this belief contrasted with the reasons given by other workers who considered themselves to be at risk. Cited by 14 of the 22 non-street workers, condom breakage was the single most common reason for their perception of heightened risk. However, none of the street workers gave condom breakage as a reason. Their most common response was that they did not always use condoms. Women working from the street have been shown in other studies to face particular difficulties in relation to practising safe sex in all sexual encounters with clients (Harcourt, 1994; Pyett and Warr, 1996).

Sexual practices and perceived risk of HIV/AIDS

Certain sex practices were viewed as being very high-risk by the vast majority of female sex workers, while others were generally considered to entail a much lower risk. The data in Table 4.7 are concerned with perceptions of risk of HIV transmission associated with oral, anal and vaginal sex in a hypothetical case where a worker was HIV positive. Overall, there appeared to exist a clear 'safety hierarchy' of sexual behaviours, with anal sex almost universally viewed as very high risk and oral sex widely viewed as low risk. Vaginal sex fell between these two sexual practices in terms of the proportion of workers who viewed it as risky. Whether or not condoms were used markedly influenced the proportion of workers who perceived each activity as risky, underlining the reliance placed on condoms as a preventive measure.

Table 4.7
Level of risk associated with sexual practices* without condoms

	None %	Slight %	Moderate %	High %
Oral sex	9	29	15	47
Anal sex	0	2	4	94
Vaginal sex	<1	7	20	72

With proper use of condoms

	None %	Slight %	Moderate %	High %
Oral sex	43	33	11	12
Anal sex	23	34	20	22
Vaginal sex	30	38	17	14

* N ranges from 196 to 197

Neither the length of time a worker had been in the industry nor her present age or type of work appeared to influence these response patterns. By contrast, the age at which the worker had entered the industry was consistently associated with response patterns. Generally speaking, the older the worker when she had entered the industry, the less likely was she to view certain practices as risky. This difference was statistically significant for anal ($p < 0.01$) and vaginal ($p < 0.01$) sex without condoms and oral sex both with ($p = 0.04$) and without ($p < 0.01$) condoms.

The issue of reliance on condoms to prevent HIV/AIDS is addressed more directly in Figure 4.2. All the women believed that condoms gave them at least 50 per cent protection and one in five women considered them to offer complete protection.

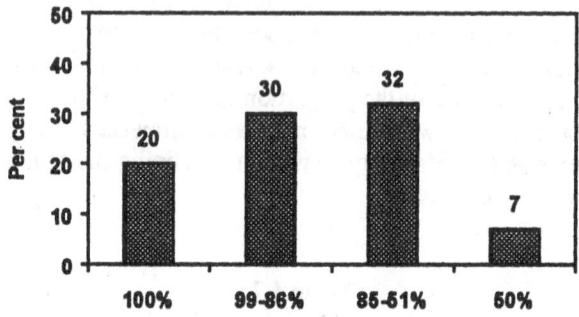

Figure 4.2 Perceived level of protection given by condoms among 199 female sex workers

Inset 4.3 provides one worker's perspective to illustrate how a reliance on condoms may be tempered by concerns about breakage or leakage. Thus, the worker states that while she has long practised safe sex she has never felt completely protected.

Inset 4.3

'I practiced safe sex while I was working for many years. I might even say that it cost me a couple of jobs when they found out I was sneaking condoms on clients because the employers weren't really thrilled about that at the time. Condoms can break and sometimes they do, no matter how careful you are. I am aware that they are not 100 per cent safe and that little bits can leak out the end of them and that sort of thing, so from that point of view I never felt 100 per cent safe.'

(INTERVIEW 1)

Table 4.8 examines in more detail the level of risk which the workers associated with a range of sexual activities. Again, the safety hierarchy in relation to sexual practices and the workers' reliance on condoms is evident. Almost the entire sample agreed that the HIV/AIDS risk associated with various forms of unprotected anal sex was very or extremely high. If a condom was used, however, around half the women thought the risk associated with anal sex, as either the active or receptive partner, was not worth worrying about. Indeed, almost one-third of the women thought it was not possible to contract HIV/AIDS from anal sex if a condom was used. Withdrawing before ejaculation was not usually thought to reduce the risk associated with anal sex and almost all workers rated this practice as at least very risky.

Vaginal sex without condoms was considered less risky than anal sex and 16 per cent of female workers believed there was little or no possibility of contracting HIV/AIDS through having unprotected vaginal intercourse. Slightly more than half the women believed the associated risk to be at least very high and more than 80 per cent acknowledged some risk. Although some women thought that withdrawal before ejaculation eliminated, or almost eliminated, the risk of HIV/AIDS associated with vaginal sex, about three quarters acknowledged some risk.

Oral sex was viewed as less risky than either anal or vaginal sex. Just over half the women (51 to 55 per cent) attached little risk to giving oral sex to a male without the use of a condom. The large majority (84 to 85 per cent) of workers thought giving oral sex to a female or receiving oral sex were low-risk practices.

Casual and tongue kissing and manual stimulation were perceived as the least risky forms of physical contact and almost the entire sample agreed there was little or no risk attached to these forms of contact. Notably, however, some 44 per cent of women thought that blood or semen on broken skin or dermatitis entailed little risk in relation to HIV infection.

Table 4.8
Levels of risk of HIV transmission associated with a range of sexual activities as perceived by female sex workers

	Not possible %	Possible but not worrying %	Risky %	Very risky %	Extremely risky %
Vaginal sex - giving, no condom	3	16	26	17	39
Vaginal sex - taking, no condom	3	13	27	18	39
Vaginal sex - giving, withdrawing before ejaculation, no condom	3	20	29	21	26
Vaginal sex - taking, withdrawing before ejaculation, no condom	3	18	30	22	26
Anal sex - giving, no condom	0	0	2	6	92
Anal sex - taking, no condom	0	0	2	5	93
Anal sex - giving, with condom	31	21	14	14	20
Anal sex - taking, with condom	32	20	14	14	21
Anal sex - taking, withdrawing before ejaculation, no condom	0	1	2	12	84
Anal sex - giving, withdrawing before ejaculation, no condom	0	1	2	12	85
Anal sex after 'fisting' without protection	<1	2	1	2	95
Oral sex - giving to male, no condom	18	33	26	7	16
Oral sex - giving to male, stopping before ejaculation, no condom	18	37	22	7	16
Oral sex - giving to woman, without protection	49	35	5	5	5
Oral sex - taking, without protection	51	34	6	5	5
Tongue kissing	55	33	9	3	0
Casual kissing	96	3	1	1	0
Manual stimulation	94	3	1	<1	0
Rimming (oral sex to anus without protection)	3	9	8	9	70
Getting blood or semen on broken skin or dermatitis	17	27	17	12	27

Perceptions of other potential risks

The workers were asked to rate the level of HIV-related risk associated with a range of other activities and situations. Table 4.9 shows a very high level of consensus regarding the risk associated with sharing uncleaned needles or those cleaned only in water: almost the entire sample agreed that these practices constituted a very or extremely high risk for HIV/AIDS. Similarly, there was almost universal agreement among workers that using public swimming pools, being coughed on, or sharing eating or drinking utensils posed little risk for HIV/AIDS.

There was less consensus about some of the other items. For example, more than half the women thought there was little or no risk of an infected mother passing on HIV/AIDS to her child either during pregnancy or through breast milk. Similarly, the workers were divided regarding perceptions of risk in relation to blood transfusions and 'haemophiliac treatment'.

Table 4.9
Level of HIV risk associated with selected activities and situations, as perceived by female sex workers

	Not possible %	Possible but not worrying %	Risky %	Very risky %	Extremely risky %
Sharing needles/syringes that have not been cleaned	0	0	1	2	97
Sharing needles/syringes that have only been rinsed with water	0	1	1	13	85
Infected mother to her child at or during birth	17	36	14	12	21
Infected mother to her child through breast milk	17	37	16	10	20
Blood transfusion	26	26	11	6	32
Haemophiliac treatment	28	28	11	5	29
Sharing eating/drinking utensils	86	10	2	<1	2
Being coughed on	92	6	1	1	0
Using public swimming pools	94	6	<1	0	0

Patterns of response to each of the items presented in Tables 4.8 and 4.9 were examined according to the worker's age, the length of time she had worked in the sex industry, her age at entry to the industry, and the type of work in which she was currently engaged. Because of the large number of statistical tests performed, it is likely that some associations reached significance by chance and, for this reason, credence can be given only to strong and consistent patterns. Overall, the above worker characteristics did not appear to influence perceptions of risk. In many cases, this is not surprising due to the high level of agreement among workers.

Nonetheless, one notable exception emerged in relation to non-condom vaginal sex. Arguably, perceptions of risk associated with vaginal sex are particularly pertinent because this service was offered by almost all the women whereas other forms of sex, such as anal sex, were offered far less frequently (see Chapter 5). Table 4.10 shows that responses to the item concerning non-condom vaginal sex varied markedly according to the age of the sex worker ($p < 0.001$). Older women were far less likely to view this as risky when compared with younger women.

Table 4.10
Risk associated with vaginal sex without condom by age of sex worker

	<20 (N=25) %	20-29 (N=110) %	30+ (N=59) %
Not possible/not worth worrying	4	10	34
Risky	24	27	27
Very/extremely risky	72	63	39

A similar pattern existed for the age the worker entered the sex industry ($p = 0.02$), with women who had started working at an older age attaching a lower level of risk to unprotected vaginal sex (Table 4.11). The length of time workers had been in the sex industry (not shown) also conformed to this pattern ($p = 0.04$). Finally, Table 4.12 considers responses according to type of work. Although the small number of street workers made it difficult to draw firm conclusions, a trend was apparent ($p = 0.03$). Private workers were generally less likely to consider unprotected vaginal sex a risky practice when compared with street and massage parlour or brothel workers.

Table 4.11
Risk associated with vaginal sex without condom by age worker entered the sex industry

	<20 (N=74) %	20-29 (N=94) %	30+ (N=26) %
Not possible/not worth worrying	11	16	35
Risky	22	31	27
Very/extremely risky	67	53	38

Table 4.12
Risk associated with vaginal sex without condom by type of work

	Brothel (N=31) %	Parlour Escort (N=46) %	Escort Agency (N=55) %	Street (N=10) %	Private (N=52) %
Not possible/not worrying	0	9	20	20	29
Risky	29	33	24	10	27
Very/extremely risky	71	59	56	70	44

The above patterns suggest that older women, who had started in the industry at a later age, who had worked in the industry for longer, and who were currently working privately tended to attach a lower risk to non-condom vaginal sex when compared with other workers. With respect to private workers, there were also earlier suggestions that they may have a lower level of anxiety about AIDS and attach a lower level of risk to some sex practices. It may be that women with these worker characteristics have a more regular and, what they may consider to be, a more select clientele. Stevens (1994) also found that some of the more experienced workers in her sample practised unsafe sex in what she described as a context of 'negotiated safety'.

Some of these worker differences may reflect some more pervasive differences with respect to perceptions about HIV risk factors. Table 4.13 shows that a worker's present age and her age at entry to the sex industry were also significantly associated with responses to the items concerning blood transfusion and haemophiliac treatment (in all cases, $p < 0.01$).

Table 4.13
Workers responding 'very' or 'extremely risky'

	Age of worker			Age entered		
	< 20 (N=24) %	20-29 (N=109) %	30+ (N=59) %	< 20 (N=72) %	20-29 (N=94) %	30+ (N=26) %
Blood transfusion	71	38	24	50	36	11
Haemophiliac treatment	58	37	19	46	33	4

Level of knowledge about HIV/AIDS

A high level of basic knowledge about HIV/AIDS was evident among the women who took part in the study. For instance, all but several workers knew that HIV/AIDS could neither be prevented by vaccine nor cured and very few workers believed they could rely on appearances to determine whether a person was HIV positive. The vast majority of women believed it was not possible to tell by looking at a person whether they had AIDS at least until the last stages of the illness. Only 9 per cent of the women reported that they would continue to work in the sex industry if they themselves were infected with HIV and the majority of these women indicated that they would do so only if condoms were used at all times.

Almost all of the women (98 per cent) understood the meaning of a positive HIV/AIDS test result. However, in isolated instances workers thought a positive result indicated non-infection (2 per cent) or were unsure as to the meaning of a positive test result (1 per cent). There appeared to be less understanding of the meaning of a negative result, especially with regard to the seroconversion period. Such gaps in knowledge about the length of time to establish non-infection are highlighted in Table 4.14. Many sex workers thought infection could be ruled out very soon after possible exposure to HIV. More than one in four women thought infection could be excluded within days of a condom breakage or other high risk event.

Table 4.14
Length of time needed to rule out HIV infection following condom breakage or other possible exposure to the AIDS virus – 186 female sex workers

	%
1 week or less	28
1 to 4 weeks	18
2 to 5 months	38
6 months	9
Longer than 6 months	4
Don't know	3

A relatively high level of uncertainty also seemed to exist in relation to the link between HIV infection and the manifestation of AIDS symptoms. Almost one third of the women were unable to answer the question while 13 per cent thought symptoms would be expected to appear within months of infection. The remaining workers thought it could take years (34 per cent) or that symptoms may not develop at all (21 per cent). Many women (52 per cent) did not know how long the HIV virus could remain outside the body, in a syringe or condom, for example. One in four workers (25 per cent) thought the virus could not exist outside the body at all, while others (17 per cent) thought it could exist for a number of hours.

Summary

The majority of female sex workers acknowledge the possibility that they could become infected with HIV but most did not think it likely, nor did they report high levels of anxiety in relation to HIV/AIDS. For the most part, this seemed to reflect a high level of condom usage among the women in our study. The women's perceptions of the safety of various sexual practices revealed a hierarchy of risks – anal sex was perceived as being most risky, oral sex as least risky and vaginal sex of intermediate risk – as well as strong reliance on condoms as a preventive measure, though some workers readily acknowledged the potential for condom breakage.

Overall, the level of knowledge about HIV/AIDS and its prevention was high suggesting that health promotion messages had reached most of the women involved in the study. Yet, there remained some areas of concern. While almost all the women had a basic understanding of HIV/AIDS and its associated risk factors, there was confusion among some workers about the meaning of a negative HIV result particularly in relation to the seroconversion period. Additionally, many women seemed unaware of the risk of HIV transmission associated with contact between semen or blood and broken skin or of the possibility of a mother passing the virus to her baby during pregnancy or breastfeeding. Around 16 per cent of women attached little or no risk to vaginal sex without a condom and they, like the small group who indicated that they did not always have ready access to condoms, are of particular concern. The next chapter deals more directly with the level of risk that may be encountered on a day to day basis by women in the sex industry.

5 Sexual practices and prevention at work

In this chapter we present an overview of what work in the sex industry in Queensland entailed for the women who took part in the study. Insights are provided into the relationship between sex workers and their clients and the types of services sex workers provide. Particular attention is given to those practices and situations which may pose significant health risks to sex workers, including those risks brought by clients to the sexual encounter.

Clients of female sex workers

The clients of most female sex workers in the study were exclusively male. Only one worker stated that she saw only female clients. Some workers (19 per cent) did see female clients but it is clear from Table 5.1 that the female workers who took part in the study had a predominantly male clientele. Perkins (1994) also found that women clients were rare and were usually wives or lovers of men who had hired a sex worker for 'doubles'.

Table 5.1
Gender breakdown of clients seen by 200 female sex workers

	Men %	Women %
All	82	1
Most	17	0
About 50/50	1	1
Some	0	17
None	1	81

The data in Table 5.2 suggest that most workers gain some sense of the occupational backgrounds of their male clients, and that these backgrounds are diverse (Inset 5.1). Again this is consistent with data presented by Perkins (1994), which suggested that sex workers' clients were quite evenly distributed in terms of social class. According to the women in our study, clients were most often business men and/or self-employed. Labourers, unskilled workers and the unemployed appeared to be underrepresented as clients relative to their numbers in the community.

Table 5.2
Occupational background of clients of 200 female sex workers
(multiple responses possible)

	%
Business man/self-employed	82
Working man/labourer	57
Office clerical	55
Tradesman	53
Professional	52
Tourists/foreigners	41
Unemployed	24
Don't know	3

Inset 5.1

> What sort of clientele would you service in the sex industry?
> A broad spectrum from politicians to factory workers ... right across the board.
> **(INTERVIEW 1)**

Tourists did not seem to make up a large proportion of clients, but this may vary according to the worker's geographical location. The 82 women who described most of their clients as tourists or foreigners indicated that the majority were from Japan (46 per cent) or elsewhere in Asia (21 per cent). A smaller proportion were said to be European or American (each 15 per cent).

Sex workers' views of clients

Workers were asked to describe, in a few words, how they felt about their clients. This elicited a range of responses which could be classified into three broad groups. Most often (47 per cent), workers were non-committal about clients, expressing no feelings either way: 'I don't think about them'; 'they are just clients'; 'they are just like anyone else, just people'; 'they are OK, I don't have any trouble'. This confirms the observation already made that sex workers tend to view their clients in a rather impersonal and strictly business way. Thus, some simply stated: 'they are money in my pocket' or 'they pay my bills'.

The second most common view of clients (35 per cent) suggested that some workers did have a certain amount of positive regard for their clients. Typical responses in this category included: 'they are usually nice'; 'they are great guys'; 'most are gentlemen'; 'they treat me lovely'; and 'I have a lot of time for my clients'.

In contrast, a smaller group of workers (18 per cent) expressed antipathy towards their clients. Some expressed hostility or aversion, making comments such as: 'I hate them all'; 'yuk'; 'they repulse me'; or 'they are mugs'. Others expressed sympathy for their clients: 'I feel sorry for them'; 'I feel sorry for them because they are sick'; and 'they are lonely people'.

Workloads of female sex workers

One issue of continuing speculation relates to the income of workers in the sex industry. Our qualitative data suggested that sex workers very quickly discover that their earning power in the industry is high relative to what they might earn in other fields of employment. Many workers also pointed out other advantages of sex work such as short hours and flexibility. In combination, these factors produced an employment opportunity that offered the chance of a more attractive lifestyle than would otherwise have been available. As Inset 5.2 shows, sex work may also be a means of ensuring a high standard of living for the worker's children.

Inset 5.2

'I was used to the income of two wages and then when I split up [with my husband] I didn't realise it would be so hard ... the children were used to a certain living standard, and I was living in a hovel and I just couldn't do it, my children weren't used to it ... I go out to work, a normal job, by the time I pay out child care, I don't see the children from seven in the morning until seven at night ... having the children with no father, why should they have no mother as well?'

(INTERVIEW 15)

Much variation was evident among workers in terms of the number of clients they saw in a given week (Table 5.3) and, even for individual workers, the number of clients was likely to vary considerably from week to week (Inset 5.3). Nonetheless, most of the women stated that the number of clients they had seen during the seven days preceding the interview was typical of the number they would see in an average week. If one were to estimate somewhere between half an hour and one hour (elapsed time) for each client contact, then just under half the sex workers typically spent no more than ten hours a week working in the industry.

Table 5.3
Number of clients seen by 200 female sex workers

	Last week %	Busiest week %	Quiet week %
0 to 5	15	5	57
6 to 10	27	9	26
11 to 15	25	11	11
16 to 20	21	24	7
21 to 25	3	9	0
26 to 50	11	36	0
51 to 100	0	7	0

Inset 5.3

> 'I can remember years ago in Brisbane, I worked in a parlour in Brunswick Street and there was only myself and one girl on one Friday night, it was a 6.00pm to 6.00am shift, and just between the two of us, we saw 40 clients. I'd say that was probably my maximum ...'
>
> **(INTERVIEW 1)**

Workers' responses with respect to how much they had earned in the last seven days ranged in amounts from $80 to $4000. Table 5.4 further examines the data concerning the income received and number of clients seen by the female sex workers. The mean weekly income and the mean income per client tended to increase with the age of the sex worker, although this trend was not statistically significant. Mean weekly income, the number of clients seen, and the average payment per client varied significantly according to type of work ($p < 0.001$). By far, the lowest weekly income is reported by street workers who not only receive a relatively low fee payment from each client, but saw significantly fewer clients than workers in other categories. Private work appeared to be most lucrative. According to our data, private workers attracted the highest fees and earned a higher average weekly income than other workers.

Information about money earned needs to be interpreted with caution in the present day context, given that the nature of the work has changed significantly since these data were collected. Anecdotal reports from SQWISI would indicate that, as fewer clients are seen at present, earnings are likely to have decreased.

Table 5.4
Mean weekly income and number of clients seen by 170 female sex workers last week by age and type of work*

	Mean income $	Mean no. clients	Mean income per client $
Age of sex worker			
< 20 years	992	15	77
20-29 years	1136	15	86
30+ years	1165	14	90
Type of work			
Massage parlour/brothel	1034	16	69
Parlour escort	1081	18	68
Escort agency	904	11	90
Street	250	6	67
Private	1577	16	112

* Excludes workers who had no clients or no income in the last week and those who completed the pilot questionnaire

Figure 5.1 shows that most of the women had at least some clients whom they saw on a regular basis (at least every six months). While sex workers tended to view regular clients as an important source of income, others pointed out disadvantages associated with 'regulars' (Inset 5.4).

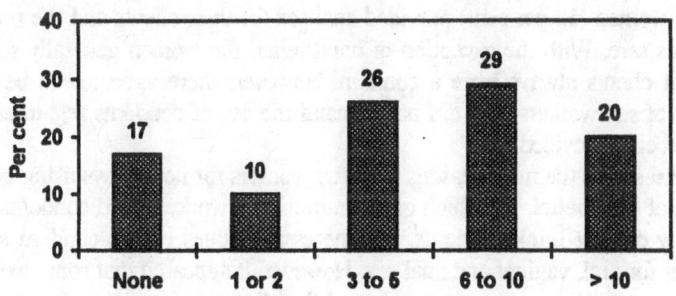

Figure 5.1 Number of regular clients of 200 female sex workers

Inset 5.4

> *What do you think about your regulars?*
> Nice guys, some of them are really strange, others are nice, some I don't like, but they bring in the bucks.
> *Do you think regulars ask for a bit more than your average guy?*
> Yes. They tend to try and develop a friendship, which just can't be done. I mean you can get on with a guy but as far as forming friendship, it's too difficult, it puts a strain on your other clients, a strain on the girl and disappointment for the client.
> **(INTERVIEW 10)**
> 'The regulars are the ones that are your bread and butter. All of them feel very pampered when they are with you, they are spoilt so that when you leave they are going to want to see you again soon.'
> **(INTERVIEW 20)**

Types of services provided by female sex workers

Inset 5.5 gives a qualitative view of the services clients expect from sex workers and what sex workers offer. In addition to sexual services, workers may also provide a source of companionship to some clients.

Drawing on the survey data, Table 5.5 provides a broader picture of the types of services provided by the sex workers as well as the prevalence of condom use for each of these services. Almost all female sex workers appear to provide hand relief, vaginal sex and oral sex and many expect that some clients will want to perform oral sex on them. Few women (12 per cent) provided anal sex for their clients and the practice of 'fisting' was rare. With the exception of hand relief, the women generally seemed to require that clients always wore a condom. However, there appeared to be a small percentage of sex workers who did not demand the use of condoms regardless of the sex service being provided.

Table 5.6 shows the main reasons given by workers for not always using condoms. In the case of hand relief, for which only a minority of workers used condoms always, most simply did not think condoms were necessary. Rates of non-condom sex were much lower for oral, vaginal and anal sex. However, it appeared that some workers on occasions agreed to sex without a condom if the client paid a higher fee. In isolated instances women stated that they had been coerced into non-condom sex and others had made concessions to clients, who were 'regulars' or had some other 'special' relationship with the worker. It was also apparent that on some occasions some women did not have ready access to condoms.

Inset 5.5

'They seem to be very keen on French and a lot of them want full French. Also a lot of them have this misconception that its alright to have full French without a condom ... one guy even went as high as $2000 for an hour not to have to wear a condom and I said this is crazy, this is absolutely crazy ... mind you I didn't see the colour of his money. He was perhaps talking through his hat.'

(INTERVIEW 1)

What services did you provide, and what cost?
Oral sex, sex, and bondage, fantasies, not anal sex. I wouldn't get into that area, yes, sort of fantasies and just the normal stuff.
What's the normal stuff?
Well, see, with just straight sex ... you go by the half hour and the hour, and so on, it's just a normal basic charge. For half an hour, it was $80 and $120, and you did just basic stuff, you know, oral and the rest of it. For anything after that you charged. I charged $30, I feel embarrassed saying this in front of you, for golden showers, you know, and depending on the amount of bondage or something like that, it would be up to maybe $100 to $200 extra.

(INTERVIEW 12)

What range of services do you provide for your clients?
Oral, part oral, full oral, or sexual intercourse, no anal sex, nothing kinky ... I'm not into the kinky stuff at all ... sometimes I get conned into giving them a massage. I'm also an escort in that I do actually go out with my clients a fair bit, I'm also a companion, I listen to the whinges, I let them cry on my shoulder ... that sort of thing.
And how much do you charge for different kinds of services?
I charge $110 for a half hour, $180 for the first hour, $140 for the second and $100 per hour after that. I've also got special rates for all night or for trips away ... prices can be flexible if the client's offering more than just a standard one or two hour job.

(INTERVIEW 3)

Do you do anal sex?
No, never. My bum is a virgin.

(INTERVIEW 15)

Table 5.5
Services provided for male clients by 179 female sex workers

	Provide service %	Use condom always %
Vaginal sex	100	94
Oral sex (with ejaculation)	79	86
Oral sex (no ejaculation)	97	77
Oral sex (from male)	68	N/A
Anal sex	12	90
Hand relief	98	15
Sex between breasts	59	17
Fisting	1	100
Fingering	21	31
Sex toys	40	93

* N/A = not applicable

Table 5.6
Reasons for not using condoms always (multiple responses possible)

	Hand relief (N=149) %	Oral sex (N=40) %	Vaginal sex (N=11) %
Not necessary	89	8	0
Client paid more	1	63	27
Regular client	1	15	0
Brothel policy	1	3	9
No condoms available	1	13	50
Forced	0	5	18
Special client relationship	1	8	10
Client couldn't 'get off' with condom	3	0	10

Inset 5.6 illustrates two worker perspectives on condom use. Although the first worker used condoms for oral and vaginal sex, she did not think they were necessary for hand relief. By contrast, the second worker used condoms in all sexual encounters with clients.

Figure 5.2 lists some of the other services provided by sex workers. Workers tend to have a particular repertoire of services, some of which may include 'specialist services' such as golden showers or bondage. Special equipment, and often specialised skills, may be required for some of these services. Some of these services do not appear to carry a high risk of transmission of disease. An example of the former type of service is massage which seems to be offered by most female workers. Inset 5.7 reflects the personal views of one worker who had a particular liking for providing bondage and discipline (B and D) services. By contrast, the second worker did not have 'the right type of mind' for bondage. Notably, the first worker was emphatic that she refused to engage in submission. This was the case for most female workers, very few of whom provided submission to clients.

Inset 5.6

> *What did you use condoms for?*
> Oral sex and sex.
> *What about hand relief? Do you use condoms for hand relief?*
> No. I allow them a little bit of comfort. You've got to be nice sometimes.
> **(INTERVIEW 12)**
> 'We are so aware, I don't even give a head job without a condom. I don't let a man's semen touch me or my hands anywhere ...'
> **(INTERVIEW 6)**

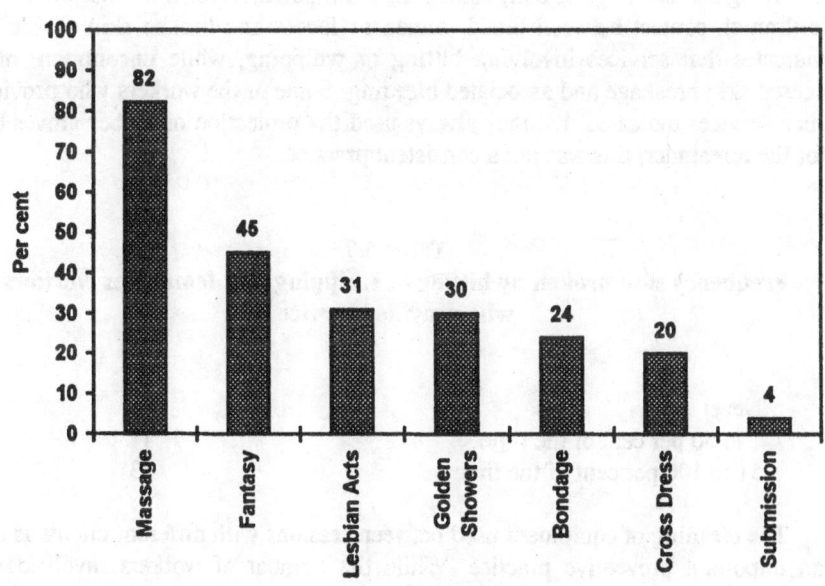

Figure 5.2   Other services provided for male clients by 179 female sex workers (multiple responses possible)

Inset 5.7

'I enjoy B and D, I have a ball. I'd rather beat the shit out of any client than screw them. It's great.'
What about submission, do you ever do that?
Not a hope in hell ... you'd have to have some impediment to allow someone to beat you to a pulp for money ... it's not worth it ... for a couple of weeks you're black and blue ...

(INTERVIEW 17)

'I've even tried bondage ... yeah, I found that very good but I don't have the heart unless I'm really angry ... I walk in there and whip, whip, whip, whip and they don't get off. So I don't have the right type of mind for bondage. I can't go in there and play a role ... Bondage is a good option for girls who don't want to participate in any sexual act ... with most bondage there's actually no sexual act that actually takes place.'

(INTERVIEW 18)

B and D services were provided by only some (26 per cent) workers and 'heavy' B and D appeared rarely to be provided. Vaginal sex was rarely offered in conjunction with either medium or heavy B and D services. In relation to these services, which may include verbal and physical abuse and degrading acts involving the exchange of body fluids, the main potential for transmission of HIV is through contact between blood, semen or faeces and broken skin. Table 5.7 indicates that services involving hitting or whipping, while uncommon, often caused skin breakage and associated bleeding. Some of the workers who provided such services indicated that they always used the protection of rubber gloves but, for the remainder, this was not a consistent practice.

Table 5.7
Frequency skin broken by hitting or whipping – 22 female sex workers who provided service

	%
Never	36
1 to 50 per cent of the time	41
51 to 100 per cent of the time	23

The cleaning of equipment used between sessions with different clients is also an important preventive practice. While the number of workers involved was small, there was some indication that the risk of transmission could be reduced through improved and more consistent methods of cleaning B and D equipment

(Table 5.8). In most instances, the equipment was cleaned using household disinfectant or soap and water.

Table 5.8
Frequency of equipment cleaning between sessions – 20 female sex workers who provided service

	%
Always	55
Most of the time	30
Rarely or never	15

Client-related risks

Concerns about the link between commercial sex and the spread of disease typically focus on the sex worker with little attention to the clients of sex workers. Yet, a recent study by Perkins, Lovejoy and Jacobsen (1966) concluded that clients constitute a significant obstacle to the sexual health of many workers. Similarly, our data suggested that clients may bring certain risks to the sexual encounter.

Clients with STDs for sexually transmitted diseases

Checking clients for visible signs of STDs has been a traditional practice in the sex industry. While its value as a preventive measure is limited because not all communicable diseases can be detected in this way, this practice may form an important opportunity for negotiation between the sex worker and client. It sets the scene for workers to be 'in charge' of the encounter, particularly in relation to the use of condoms and the education of clients about sexual health matters. The majority of workers reported that they always checked their clients for signs of sexually transmitted diseases. Only 12 per cent of women reported that they did not check their clients in every sexual encounter. When asked who had taught them to do this 48 per cent indicated that it was another sex worker while a further 24 per cent had been taught by other industry workers, such as parlour owners or receptionists (Table 5.9).

Table 5.9
**Source of information about checking clients for signs of STDs –
187 female sex workers**

	%
Another worker	48
Parlour owner or receptionist	24
Doctor, nurse, STD clinic staff	11
Read about it	6
SQWISI	3
Other	8

It is interesting that these preventive strategies appear to be learnt in an apprenticeship-type mode, with relatively few workers having obtained such information from health professionals or support groups such as SQWISI. This raises the possibility that skills acquired in this context may not be learnt properly and that workers may learn accurate as well as inaccurate strategies for protecting themselves from disease.

In Inset 5.8, one worker describes her involvement in providing informal 'on the job' training to fellow massage parlour workers. This kind of comprehensive training is less likely to occur where in-house services are uncommon, as is currently the case in Queensland. The second worker emphasises the educational needs of sex workers and, in particular, the importance of open dialogue on this issue. As this worker points out, without educational information that is both accessible and appropriate, knowledge about risks and preventive strategies is likely to be passed on in a haphazard way, failing to reach those who need it most.

Inset 5.8

> 'There's three girls in Melbourne who are actually sent around to all the parlours as needed, to do training massages. I was one and I would actually get the girl to give me the half-hour service and then I would turn around and teach her where she went wrong ... how to put the condom on with her mouth, what to look for if the client wants to be doggy, make sure he's not flicking the end of the condom or this type of thing.'
>
> (INTERVIEW 13)
>
> 'We need more information, we need to be able to go to people without fear of having our names in public and people pointing at us in public, and we need to be treated like anybody else as far as educational needs ... an industry that is being pushed underground through legal reasons, through laws, through police, it just makes it harder to educate people on the dangers involved and the information doesn't quite get through to where it should be getting through.'
>
> (INTERVIEW 5)

Most workers (61 per cent) had been exposed to clients showing signs of STDs (Table 5.10). Only 32 per cent of workers said they had seen no evidence of STDs on clients while a further 7 per cent were unsure. The STDs most often seen in clients were warts and herpes. When workers encountered a client whom they suspected of having an STD, most refused to see that client. However, this was not always the case. Table 5.11 shows that a small number of workers saw the client as usual or compromised by offering an alternative service.

Table 5.10
STDs seen on clients as reported by 135 female sex workers
(multiple responses possible)

	%
Warts	53
Herpes	34
Gonorrhoea	17
Thrush	9
Syphilis	4
Trichomoniasis	1
Not sure	7

Table 5.11
Response of 131 female sex workers to client suspected of having an STD

	%
Refuse to see client	81
Offer an alternative service (e.g., hand relief)	12
Do as usual	7

Client intravenous drug use

The health of sex workers may be endangered, not only by high-risk sexual practices and the sexual health of their clients, but also by client practices such as intravenous drug use. Some 17 per cent of workers reported having clients whom they knew to be using injecting drugs (Table 5.12), but this figure undoubtedly would be higher as one third of workers did not know if any of their clients were users. Clearly, for a sizeable number of sex workers, the use of intravenous drugs by clients poses an additional risk to their health.

Table 5.12
Knowledge of client's use of injecting drugs – 197 female sex workers

	%
Yes	17
No	50
Don't know	33

About two thirds of the women (61 per cent) indicated that they would provide the service as usual if they suspected or knew that their client was injecting drugs. Comparison of Tables 5.13 and 5.11 suggests that workers may be much less likely to refuse a client who injects drugs (24 per cent) than one thought to have an STD (81 per cent). While the majority of sex workers appeared to be acutely aware of the known risks of transmission in relation to STDs, they may be less well-informed about the additional risks brought to sexual encounters by clients who are intravenous drug users.

Table 5.13
Response of 162 female sex workers to client suspected of injecting drugs

	%
Do as usual	61
Refuse to see client	24
Offer an alternative service (e.g., hand relief)	15

Client inducements for non-condom sex

Our data suggested that, among female sex workers, condoms were widely accepted as a means of reducing the transmission of disease. In line with this, the majority of workers claimed always to use condoms for those forms of sex which were likely to constitute the highest risk (see Table 5.5). Nonetheless, we have also seen (Table 5.6) that there may be situations where workers are asked by clients to provide non-condom sex. They may be offered extra money to do so and, in some cases, they may have difficulty negotiating with clients on this issue.

Table 5.14 examines the extent to which sex workers in the study were offered extra money for sex without a condom. These broad estimates of the frequency with which such offers were made indicated that in any week a majority of female sex workers are offered extra money to have unprotected sex.

Table 5.14
Times each week 197 female sex workers offered more money for non-condom sex

	%
Never	27
Once	18
2 to 5 times	32
6 to 10 times	15
More than 10 times	4
Not stated	4

Table 5.15 presents information about the dollar amounts that sex workers had been offered for non-condom sex. These represent an extraordinary diversity of amounts, but it must be noted that there was no confirmatory evidence that such amounts were actually paid. Indeed, informal discussions with workers suggested that while clients may make apparently rash offers of money for non-condom sex, few follow such offers through by actually producing the money. Many of the sex workers we interviewed seemed sceptical that such amounts would be forthcoming. One is left

with the impression that while many clients would prefer non-condom sex they are only prepared to pay modest amounts to receive this type of service. Even so, client resistance to condom use would appear to pose a threat to consistent condom use for at least some sex workers.

Table 5.15
Most money offered to 200 female sex workers for non-condom sex

	%
Up to $50	8
$51 to $199	27
$200 to $499	27
$500 to $999	17
$1000 or more	17
Not stated	3

Table 5.16 suggests that few women would accept extra money for non-condom sex though it is of course impossible to verify these responses. A small number of workers who said that they always declined extra money for sex without a condom admitted after the survey interview that they had accepted such offers when large sums of money had been involved.

Table 5.16
Response to offer of extra money for non-condom sex by 138 female sex workers who had been offered financial inducement

	%
Talk the client into using the condom	66
Provide an alternative service	16
Refuse to see the client	13
Do the service as requested by client	3
Accept the money and do the job	1

For the most part, however, workers were emphatic about using condoms and were experienced in convincing clients to use them. Illustrative of this are the observations of two sex workers presented in Inset 5.9 as well as the responses in Table 5.17.

Table 5.17
Clients' usual response to insistence on condom use – 195 female sex workers

	%
Usually they are okay, they just use the condom anyway	74
They use the condom, but grudgingly	23
Refuse to see the worker	3

Inset 5.9

> *Do you use a condom?*
> Yes I do. I think my life is worth more than $150.
> **(INTERVIEW 21)**
> 'I have got a customer that hates wearing a condom and I spend half an hour, maybe three quarters of an hour, to convince him to wear one and it is a hassle but no condom no sex.'
> **(INTERVIEW 19)**

Consistent with other Australian data (Harcourt and Philpot, 1990) our data indicated that the clients of sex workers, the workers themselves (see below), and their employers had become increasingly accepting of condom use over time as a result of publicity about AIDS and other STDs. Of the 90 women in our study who were working in the sex industry prior to 1987, the majority (96 per cent) thought clients were now more willing to use condoms.

Table 5.18 gives a broad indication of actual patterns of condom use prior to 1987. While these data need to be treated tentatively due to the possibility of selective recall, some trends were apparent. Condoms were rarely used in non-work sexual relationships which is in clear contrast to sex with clients. Even so, the majority of women reported that they did not always use condoms with clients prior to 1987 and at this time almost half the women (42 per cent) did not use condoms at all.

Table 5.19 examines the extent to which publicity about AIDS led to changes in condom usage. The data indicate that, for sex with clients, most women began using condoms or using them more often at this time. Fewer women reported making any changes in their private lives, an issue that is taken up in greater detail in the next chapter. In most cases (79 per cent), workers had made a personal decision to change their patterns of condom use presumably as a result of widespread publicity about AIDS. Less often, workers stated that they had been influenced by advice from their STD clinic (12 per cent) or by changes to management policy (9 per cent).

Table 5.18
Frequency with which female sex workers used condoms before 1987

	With clients (N=75)* %	With partners (N=172)* %
Never	42	86
Occasionally	5	3
Half of the time	9	2
Usually	9	1
Always	35	8

* Excludes women who were not working and/or did not have a partner before 1987

Table 5.19
Changes made to sexual practices around 1987 or when first aware of AIDS

	With clients (N=75)* %	With partners (N=172)* %
No changes	39	72
Started using condoms	37	21
Increased condom use	17	4
Other/not stated	7	3

* Excludes women not working before 1987 and/or with no partner

The qualitative interviews also provided much evidence of an increasing awareness of the need for protected sex over time. Inset 5.10 presents the observations of two sex workers in relation to these apparent attitudinal and behavioural shifts. At the same time, the data indicated that such change has not been universal and that a substantial number of clients preferred not to use condoms and would not use them if it were not for the insistence of the sex worker. Two of the workers in Inset 5.10 pointed to the role of employers in the sex industry in influencing whether or not condoms are used by workers. In some instances management policy was such that condoms were not to be used unless at the client's request. However, discussion with sex workers who took part in the study suggested that this was likely to be far less common now than it may have been in the past.

Inset 5.10

Do you always use condoms?
Oh yes, for many, many years. When I first started in the industry it was not tolerated or allowed by employers ... you would not have lasted in the business if you were one in a thousand girls insisting on condoms, you would have had no clients. The very odd client would ask to use a condom, but aside from that it was simply not accepted. But some years back it became more accepted.
Can you tell me when condoms became more accepted?
I'm just trying to think. For me it changed as soon as I caught gonorrhoea, that was the end of it for me. I didn't want to know about no condoms then, but I would say probably in the last 12 years or something like that there has been a perception. But it certainly hasn't been with everybody and it has slowly been increasing that it is a must.
There wasn't one particular time when suddenly things changed dramatically?
No, it's been a slow thing, there are always the places of employment that have held out to the bitter end, thinking they'd get more clients if they didn't insist on the clients wearing condoms.

(INTERVIEW 1)

Do you think clients' views on condoms have changed recently?
Yes, they have. But you've still got the odd few that say 'Look, I just can't stand it, I can't handle it, I can't keep my erection, I have problems with ejaculation with a condom'. I'm sorry, we can't help you unless you do.
So not so many try to get away without using them?
No. It's very good. Actually, clients are better behaved now than they have ever been.

(INTERVIEW 11)

'Until the AIDS virus came out, the only time a worker would use condoms was if the clients requested them ... I was taught and a lot of older working girls were taught how to check men for possible STDs but that seems to have gone out the window and especially now, that condoms are so widely used they're not bothering to check them because they're feeling like "Oh well, we're using condoms". I know there was a period of time when I wouldn't employ people that always used condoms because it was bad for business. Your business would drop right down to nothing if you insisted on condoms because the clients just don't like wearing them ... Well there's still some that don't like it and they try to wangle their way out of it and offer more money and there's probably girls that still will do it ... for more money or to encourage their own clientele to build up and everything ... but it's getting easier all the time.'

(INTERVIEW 16)

Most women (83 per cent) stated that they did not find it difficult to persuade clients to use condoms. However, 16 per cent did have difficulty at least sometimes. Responses to an open-ended question suggested that it was the ensuing argument with clients and the 'hassle' involved that created difficulties for most of these women. Some stated that clients who were drunk were a particular source of difficulty in this regard. In other instances, workers had observed cultural differences among clients with respect to condom use (see Inset 5.11). It is usual practice for workers themselves to put the condom on their clients. Almost all the women (91 per cent) stated that they always put the condom on the client themselves.

Inset 5.11 also provides insight into the types of strategies sex workers may use in convincing clients to use condoms and again highlights that, since the AIDS awareness campaign, condom use has become more acceptable to many male clients. The first worker would point out to the client that if she made an exception for him, he was not to know that she had not done the same for other clients. The second worker saw herself as bolstering 'the male ego' by stressing that she was concerned with his protection. In both of these cases, the worker sought to increase the client's awareness of the risk he was taking by not using a condom.

Inset 5.11

> 'Oh, you get the odd person who says "Oh, come on let me off" ... and I usually sit down and say "If I let you off that means I let the guy before you off and the guy before him and the guy before him" and they start to think "Oh God this is awful" and they go "Okay, where's the condom?" They change their mind because they can see it's a big sloppy circle that goes the other way.'
>
> **(INTERVIEW 17)**
>
> *Are clients concerned about STDs?*
> Not very concerned ... most clients never had an STD from a worker. So they don't see that there's any problem ... some are bold enough to think that the worker uses condoms for their protection ... when the worker uses it for her own of course ... let them think that though ... it builds up the male ego. Success in this industry is based on recognising that male ego and building it up and pushing it along a bit.
>
> **(INTERVIEW 14)**
>
> *Are there many men that don't mind wearing condoms?*
> Not many, no. No a lot don't like wearing them ... when I first started insisting on condoms, that was before the AIDS scare, there were more who refused to wear them, and sometimes you can sneak them on. A lot of times you can sneak a condom on ... I've been doing it for a long time.
>
> **(INTERVIEW 12)**
>
> *So what specific regulations do you think need to be enforced by law?*
> Condom use.
> ...
> Oh, Turks, Greeks, Lebanese and Indians, and of course Vietnamese, just won't wear them and that's it. Australians are pretty good, pretty good ... you get your odd one.
> *And what did you do when you had a client that wouldn't ... well haggled a bit too much?*
> If I had one that was really haggling, I put it on with my mouth anyway, I can talk with a condom in my mouth, they don't even know I've got it. If they bring up the subject of a condom, or change the subject, I never say no to a client because you're going to have an aggro booking ... I would just change the subject and get them interested in something else, nine times out of ten I'd have that condom on without them even knowing it ...
>
> **(INTERVIEW 13)**

The next two workers had adopted a rather different strategy, 'sneaking' the condom on without the client necessarily being aware that a condom is being used. This appeared to be a skill used by more experienced workers. While having potential value as a strategy for avoiding the transmission of disease, it is one that would seem to be less desirable than those based on open communication between the sex worker and her client. It could, for example, in some instances, lead to risks of a different kind for sex workers by provoking a hostile reaction in clients. Some workers drew attention to the notion of condom use being made compulsory by law. Presumably, many sex workers would welcome efforts to enforce the mandatory use of condoms because it would take the onus off them to persuade and convince clients of the need for protected sex.

Condom breakage

Table 5.20 indicates that while most workers had experienced condom breakages, such events occurred relatively infrequently. Nevertheless, the fact is they do occur and, if we extrapolate from the number of clients seen per worker (see Table 5.3), then they occurred on a not infrequent basis for many sex workers.

Table 5.20
Frequency of condom breakage with clients - 200 female sex workers

	%
1 in 10 clients (or more often)	1
1 in 20 clients	5
1 in 100 clients	9
Less often than 1 in 100 clients	48
Never	38

Table 5.21 shows the main reasons indicated by workers as causing condom breakages. The indication was that the generous use of lubricant is effective in reducing the likelihood of breakages.

Table 5.21
Reasons for condom breakage with clients - 122 female sex workers
(multiple responses possible)

	%
No/not enough lubricant	43
Client's penis too large	33
Rough sex	31
Client breaks condom deliberately	9
Bad batch of condoms	8
Don't know	10

This was also suggested by the worker in Inset 5.12 who had experienced condom breakages on many occasions but appeared to have reduced the frequency with which they occurred by using lubricant. Most women in the study did in fact report using a lubricant although this depended to some extent on the service being provided. The effective use of lubricant would appear to warrant some attention as a preventive strategy.

Inset 5.12

Did you ever have condoms breaking?
Yes.
About how frequently would they break?
A lot. If I was to see ten clients a night, you could guarantee that five or six of them would break, but that's only because they're eager beavers and they just go really hard, and they don't give you any time to use the wet stuff and so they break only through pressure, nothing else.
And what made the difference, using lube?
Oh yes, if you get a chance to put it on. You know, like you can put it on first, but if they're going for longer than ten or fifteen minutes it dries out and because you're not enjoying yourself, you're not lubricating yourself and so they break.

(INTERVIEW 12)

Summary

The female sex workers offered a range of services to an almost exclusively male clientele. The number of clients seen in a typical week varied but usually ranged from 6 to 20. Older private workers tended to attract a higher fee for services provided. Vaginal sex, oral sex, hand relief and massage were offered by all or most workers. Other services such as anal sex or bondage, for example, were offered by far fewer workers.

The data indicated that the majority of female sex workers had adopted the consistent use of condoms for services which carry the highest risk of HIV transmission and that clients' receptiveness to their use had increased. The impression gained overall is that, with the appropriate level of skill, many workers are able to take a leading role with clients in negotiating the use of condoms and also in ensuring that the condom is worn during sex. Negotiations with clients about the use of condoms is an important skill to acquire, and the need for training of workers in this area is indicated. As condoms are usually put on clients by workers themselves, appropriate skills for doing this should also be part of this education. Supportive management policies with respect to the use of condoms were regarded by workers as highly valuable.

Despite the apparently high level of condom use, condom breakage and financial inducement for non-condom sex are of some concern. While relatively infrequent, condom breakages are likely to be a reality for most sex workers in time. The data suggested that the incidence of breakage could be reduced and minimised with the effective use of lubricant. About three quarters of the workers reported being offered more money for non-condom sex on at least a weekly basis. Most seemed to resist these financial incentives but the minority of workers who do not are at potential risk. Again, these issues have implications for sex worker education strategies.

The practice of checking clients' genitalia for signs of STDs was common. Although this practice cannot be relied on as a preventive measure in itself, it is a useful part of the negotiation with a client about safe sex and provides the opportunity for discussion about health issues with clients. These skills need to be taught by other more experienced sex workers, who ideally are supported in this role by health professionals who specialise in sexual health. Other risks which may be associated with clients are difficult to assess. However, there were indications that a significant proportion of clients may pose a risk to sex workers because they are intravenous drug users.

6 Non-work risk practices

The intention of this chapter is to present a more complete picture of the health risks to which female sex workers may be exposed. While much emphasis has so far been placed on health risks directly related to the provision of sexual services to paying clients, sex workers may also be exposed to risks in their private lives. Such risks may derive from unprotected sex with private partners and the use of alcohol and other drugs.

During the pilot phase of the study, it became apparent that while workers were comfortable answering detailed questions about sexual practices at work, they regarded similar questions about sexual relationships in their private lives as intrusive. Accordingly, questions were modified to enable a more sensitive approach to the investigation of these issues. The separation of work and private lives proved to be a significant issue with regard to considerations of safe sex practices with steady partners.

Non-work sex partners

Just over half the women (55 per cent) had a regular non-work sexual partner whom they saw at least monthly. Of these relationships, more than half (59 per cent) were of at least one year's standing and about one third (32 per cent) were of at least three years' standing. The workers' private partners, like their clients, were usually male (90 per cent) but some (10 per cent) had a female partner. Outside of work, the majority of workers did not have multiple partners. Just over one third (38 per cent) reported more than one sex partner in the last year. Seventeen per cent reported having more than two partners in the last year.

Condom use with private partners

Table 6.1 shows the extent to which the women used condoms with regular and casual non-paying sex partners in the year prior to the study interview. These figures contrast sharply with rates of condom usage with clients as presented in the previous chapter (see Table 5.5). Here it was shown that 94 per cent of women reported that they always used condoms for vaginal sex with clients. However, as Table 6.1 shows, only 22 per cent of women reported using condoms always or most of the time with their regular partner. This lower rate of condom usage also extended to casual private partners, although condoms seemed more likely to be used with casual than with regular partners. These data are consistent with other studies (Day and Ward, 1990; Dorfman, Derish, and Cohen, 1992; Harcourt and Philpot, 1990) which indicate that many female sex workers take a more cautious approach with clients than with private partners.

Table 6.1
Frequency of condom use with non-work partners

	Regular partner (N=105) %	Other partners (N=74) %
Not applicable (female partner)	10	1
Never	63	53
Not used often	2	0
Sometimes	4	5
Most of the time	6	4
All the time	16	37

Table 6.2 suggests that the lower rates of condom use with private partners represented a strategy used by the sex workers to differentiate between paid and private sexual activities. In a situation where paid work involves the performance of numerous and varied sexual acts there appears to be a need to give particular meaning to sex performed for emotional rather than for financial reasons. To require a regular partner to wear a condom appears to suggest that the sex worker is treating him as a client. This seems to be unacceptable to either the sex worker or her regular partner. The use or non-use of condoms therefore takes on a certain symbolic significance. Non-condom sex seems to symbolise the emotional attachment that a sex worker feels for her partner while the use of condoms tends to indicate a sexual transaction free of emotional attachment.

Table 6.2
Main reasons given by 82 female sex workers for not always using condoms with regular partner (multiple responses possible)

	%
I see it as an intimate relationship and I don't want to use condoms in my private life	62
I use condoms at work all the time	46
My partner dislikes condoms	17
My partner doesn't have other sex partners	13
My partner has regular STD checks	6
I'm on the pill	4
I get more gratification	2

A second perspective on the lower rates of condom usage with private partners involves the issue of power in sexual relationships. Some evidence suggests that, for a variety of reasons, women generally may not feel they are in a position to insist on condom use in their intimate relationships. Leonardo and Chrisler (1992), for example, suggested that sex workers were likely to have more power in their work relationships than in their private sexual relationships. This theme was not explicitly addressed in the present survey, but is one which may warrant further exploration.

Risks associated with private partners

In view of the low rate of condom use with private partners, sex workers may be at risk for HIV infection and other STDs if those partners engage in unsafe practices such as unprotected sex with other people or intravenous drug use.

The workers in the study were asked whether their regular sex partner had had sex with other people in the last year. Answers to this question would need to be treated tentatively as, presumably, some workers may not have been aware that their partner was having sex with other people. However, 26 per cent of the female workers reported that such events had occurred and a further 15 per cent indicated they did not know whether their regular partner had engaged in sex with other people in the last year. In other words, almost half the women who had a regular partner acknowledged the possibility that their partner may have been having sex with other people. Moreover, only 26 per cent of those women thought their partner would always have practiced safe sex with other partners.

Table 6.3 is concerned with injecting drug use among regular or other non-paying sex partners. While answers to this question would again need to be treated with caution as some persons may inject without their partner's knowledge, some 17 per cent of sex workers knew that their partners used injecting drugs. As observed earlier in relation to clients (see Table 5.14), many women may not appreciate the level of risk associated with sexual partners who are injecting drug users.

Table 6.3
Injecting drug use of sex partners last year

	Regular partner (N=104) %	Casual partners (N=72) %
Yes	17	7
No	80	78
Don't know	3	15

Drug and alcohol use

In many settings, sex work is associated with the use of alcohol and other psychoactive drugs and, accordingly, the use of such substances has been found to be relatively high among some groups of workers (De Graaf, Vanwesenbeeck, Van Zessen, Straver and Visser, 1995; Harcourt and Philpot, 1990; Perkins, 1994; Plant, 1990). While drug and alcohol misuse represents a significant health issue in itself, the disinhibiting effects of many substances may also lead to a greater propensity to engage in high-risk behaviours including unprotected sex. The use of intravenous drugs is also directly associated with the risk of HIV infection through the sharing of needles and syringes.

The data presented below provide a broad estimate of the prevalence of licit and illicit drug use among the female sex workers in our study. The proportion of workers who had ever used a variety of substances is shown together with the proportion who had used in the week preceding the study interview. This second figure therefore provides a general indication of rates of current use. As in most community surveys of substance use, the reliability of reporting must be questioned in view of a known tendency for respondents to under-report their actual usage. Moreover, in the present study, some respondents chose not to complete this section and it may be that these workers were more likely to be drug users. Overall then, it is probably reasonable to expect that the figures reported are fairly conservative estimates of rates of substance use among sex workers.

Legal substances

Table 6.4 indicates that cigarette smoking is very common among female sex workers. About three quarters of the women had used tobacco, and all of these women were current smokers. This rate is much higher than that reported in the general community where 25 to 40 per cent of women aged between 18 and 44 are current smokers (Australian Bureau of Statistics, 1992). It is, however, a rate that is comparable with other data collected from female sex workers in Australia (Harcourt and Philpot, 1990).

Table 6.4
Legal substance use by 172 female sex workers

	Ever used %	Used last week %
Tobacco	74	74
Alcohol	72	57
Tranquillisers	8	3
Anti-depressants	3	1
Pain killers	3	1

By contrast, the proportion of workers who had consumed alcohol appeared to be no higher than that observed in the wider community. Data from the National Health Survey (Australian Bureau of Statistics, 1992) indicated that 55 per cent of women aged 18 to 44 had consumed alcohol in the week preceding the survey. This figure is almost identical to the 57 per cent of sex workers who had used alcohol in the week prior to their involvement in the present study. Without data concerning the quantity consumed and the frequency of consumption, it was not possible to determine whether those sex workers who consumed alcohol did so at higher levels than women in the general population. Among the female sex workers in our study, the use of prescription and other over-the-counter drugs such as tranquillisers, anti-depressants and pain killers appeared to be uncommon.

Illegal substances

Overall, our data indicated that the use of some illicit drugs was more widespread among sex workers than in the general community and, again, these patterns are broadly comparable with those reported in other studies of female sex workers in Australia (Harcourt and Philpot, 1990; Perkins, 1994). Table 6.5 indicates that 61 per cent of the women had used cannabis and most of them had done so during the last week. This figure is relatively high when compared with data from a National Drug Household Survey conducted by the National Drug Strategy (1993), which indicated that about 33 per cent of Queensland women had ever used cannabis. Among the female sex workers, cannabis was used only marginally less than alcohol in the week before the study interview.

Table 6.5
Illegal substance use by 172 female sex workers

	Ever used %	Used last week %
Cannabis	61	51
Amphetamines	23	9
Heroin	14	6
Cocaine	11	1
Methadone	8	5
Ecstasy	8	2
Hallucinogens	6	1
Inhalants	2	0
Barbiturates	1	1

Amphetamines were the next most commonly used illicit drugs. Almost one in four workers reported having ever used amphetamines compared with 7 to 11 per cent of women under 40 in the wider community (National Drug Strategy, 1993). However, only 9 per cent of the workers had used amphetamines in the last week suggesting a pattern of occasional, rather than regular, use.

An estimated 14 per cent of the women had ever used heroin and 6 per cent had done so in the previous week. This rate is considerably higher than the 1 per cent reported in the community (National Drug Strategy, 1993). Cocaine use was also relatively high and this perhaps relates to its stimulant effect for women working at night. Eleven per cent of the workers, compared with 1 to 3 per cent of women in the community (National Drug Strategy, 1993) had ever used cocaine though only 1 per cent of workers had used it in the last week. Small percentages of the female workers reported that they had used methadone, ecstasy, hallucinogens, inhalants or barbiturates but very few had used these drugs in the last week.

Intravenous drug use

The use of injecting drugs is of particular concern given the high level of HIV-risk associated with the use of shared needles. Indeed, in most developed countries, including Australia, HIV infection among female sex workers is more likely to be attributable to intravenous drug use than to sexual contacts (Estebanez, Fitch and Najera, 1993; Plant, 1990).

Inset 6.1 illustrates how the working environments of some sex workers may be conducive to drug-taking, including the use of injecting drugs, a point which is discussed further shortly. The worker in this instance indicates that groups of workers routinely had 'party hits' and that the sharing of needles and syringes was widespread. However, like most other workers in the study who had previously shared needles, she had discontinued this practice once she had become aware of the health risks involved.

Inset 6.1

> *What about sharing needles?*
> Yes, that happens ... we used to have what we call party hits, especially in this one parlour where I worked, we used to lock the place up and all sit around and have what you call party hits, and we all used to share the same needle until it got a little bit blunt.
> *Was the management aware of what you were doing?*
> Oh, probably, yes ... and I'd share needles if I was hanging out and couldn't get a needle, it was usually early in the morning or late at night, I couldn't get a fit from anywhere, so I'd just borrow somebody else's. I cleaned it with disinfectant once because I thought it was infected, and I nearly poisoned myself ... this is a few years ago now.
> *At what stage did you stop sharing [needles]?*
> ... I was more worried about hepatitis than AIDS, maybe it's a strange thing but I was quite worried. That's why I stopped sharing needles because I was worried about hepatitis.
> **(INTERVIEW 12)**

One in four female sex workers reported having used injecting drugs on at least one occasion (Table 6.6). Of those women, almost half (41%) had shared a needle and syringe (Table 6.7).

Table 6.6
Percentage of 200 female sex workers who had ever injected a drug or other substance

	%
Yes	25
No	75

This compared with a figure of 2 per cent of women in the general population (Commonwealth Department of Health, Housing, Local Government and Community Services, 1993). Street workers were significantly more likely to have used injecting drugs as were women who had been in the industry longer and had started at a younger age ($p < 0.001$ in each instance).

Table 6.7
Female sex workers who had ever shared a needle and syringe
(51 women who had used injecting drugs)

	%
Yes	41
No	59

The data suggested that needle sharing had become less widespread since the HIV-related risks associated with this practice had been publicised. Of the 21 women who had ever shared drug-injecting equipment, six (29 per cent) had done so within the last two months. The remaining women had shared equipment during the last year or two (33 per cent) or less recently (38 per cent). The indiscriminate sharing of drug-taking equipment appeared to be uncommon. Most workers who had ever shared needles, reported that they had only done so with selected individuals and usually (71 per cent) only with a regular partner. Others (29 per cent) had shared needles with close friends but none reported having usually shared with casual partners, clients or other people at work.

Most of the women who used injecting drugs always used new needles and fits (60 per cent) while most (37 per cent) of the remaining women always cleaned equipment using the 2x2x2 bleach and water method. About half (48 per cent) the injecting drug users regularly used a needle exchange.

The association between sex work and drug use

Both our quantitative and qualitative data suggested that workers in the sex industry are a group likely to experience problems with drug use to a greater extent than the population as a whole. Fifteen per cent of the female workers had sought treatment for a drug or alcohol problem at some stage. Of that group of workers, 57 per cent had done so in relation to heroin.

There is no single explanation for the higher rates of drug use among some groups of sex workers. In some cases, working in the sex industry is likely to lead to higher levels of exposure to and subsequent use of drugs. Women may use these substances because they work in an environment where drugs may be both relatively easy to acquire and more widely used than in some other work settings. They may also use a variety of drugs as a coping mechanism to deal with stresses that are inherent in their work situation. In other instances, drug-taking may predate entry to the industry with sex work offering a source of income to support an existing drug habit. Consistent with this, some workers (40 per cent) in the study reported that their use of alcohol and drugs had increased since they had entered the sex industry, while slightly more (56 per cent) reported that their use had remained unchanged. The remaining 4 per cent of women stated that their use had decreased since entering the sex industry.

Inset 6.2 presents several perspectives on drug use among sex workers which emerged during the qualitative interviews. We see that workers may use drugs for a combination of reasons including the need to 'fix' their mind or to stay awake during long shifts extending into the early hours of the morning. Others point out the social nature of the work and the fact that alcohol and other drugs may be freely available to workers and clients often to promote what the second respondent in Inset 6.2 describes as a 'party-like' atmosphere.

Inset 6.2

'... there's a link between drugs and prostitution, because the job's a really hard job to do and you need something to fix your mind ...'

(INTERVIEW 12)

'It was like a great big party. There was a room full of people, just like a party. And of course there was boredom too. You start at four in the afternoon and you have to be there until four in the morning.'

(INTERVIEW 14)

'... to work I got out of it, to get out of it I had to work ... I refused to ever work for drugs. There are some things, I mean it was bad enough working let alone screwing for drugs ... I made good money so I never needed to sleep with someone for drugs.'

How did you spend the money that you earned?
On drugs. Mostly on drugs. Clothes sometimes.

(INTERVIEW 12)

Do you think workers use alcohol more, perhaps because it's part of the ritual or work?
No more than a business man who'll sit down and have a drink with business companions. I think there's certain jobs where socialisation is part of the work.
So you don't drink much?
No. Definitely not. I'd just stuff up.
What about pills?
Oh you might get into the No-Doze occasionally. Around 3am you might find it hard to stay awake so you might take a No-Doze or you might get into the coke [coca-cola] or the coffee ... I drink about five litres of coke a day ... it helps me stay awake.

(INTERVIEW 17)

It is important to acknowledge, however, that many sex workers do not use drugs and that, in some organised settings, the use of drugs may be actively discouraged. Our data indicated that it was not unusual for illicit drugs to be banned from work premises. In Inset 6.3, for example, a proprietor of a brothel reports that she did not allow drugs into her establishment and one gains the impression from this and other qualitative data that many establishments have this policy.

Inset 6.3

> *What about drug use, what's your experience of drug use in the industry?*
> During my time as a parlour owner I had a very good working relationship with the Police prior to Fitzgerald. All I had to do was pick up the phone, any girl that was caught on my premises, either came from a job stoned or came to work stoned, they were finished for the night and if it happened again they were finished completely.
> *What sort of drugs did you see being used?*
> Never, not in my place. Never. I ran a drug-free house.
> **(INTERVIEW 11)**
> 'Unfortunately, when heroin comes into a parlour ... it creeps through ... like a fog. It creeps right through the place. You can have one worker there on heroin and in a matter of no time you have a heap of them ... because it'll either attract the ones that have been into it and aren't using it anymore or it'll attract the new ones that were probably headed that way anyway ... and it's quite horrible ... but, unfortunately once they start using IV drugs, because they're earning instant cash all the time, they're less likely to be recreational users and more likely to get habits, because they can afford to.'
> **(INTERVIEW 16)**
> '... they're either too far into drugs or they come to work totally drunk, so they're sacked. There's only so many parlours you can go around before word gets around you're not a good worker. So that's one reason why some people go out and work on the streets or people will set up on their own.'
> **(INTERVIEW 13)**

As the last worker in Inset 6.3 points out, those workers who use drugs are more likely to be marginalised from organised work settings and forced into street work where their problems are likely to be compounded.

Summary

Potential risks to the health of sex workers extend beyond those encountered in relation to sexual practices with paying clients. Just over half the workers had a regular private partner and a minority (17 per cent) reported having more than one non-work partner, other than their regular partner, during the previous year. Workers appear to have a rather different view of sexual relationships with partners in their private lives when compared with sex with clients in the work context. Only 22 per cent stated that they used condoms all or most of the time with a regular private partner. This much lower rate of condom use when compared with paying partners appears to be a strategy for distinguishing between a client at work and a partner in the woman's private life.

Given the low rate of condom use in private relationships, it is of concern that some partners appear to be at high risk of HIV exposure through either having sex with other partners where it is unlikely that condoms are used and/or through the use of injecting drugs. This is also of concern with respect to the small group of women who had multiple partners during the year.

The use of some licit and illicit drugs was relatively widespread among the female sex workers. For legal substances, the extremely high levels of tobacco use (three quarters of the workers were current smokers) are of concern. Cannabis use was also prevalent, with half the women reporting use in the week before the study interview. Heroin usage rates of 14 per cent (ever used) and 6 per cent (used last week) were higher than found in the general population. In terms of HIV, this is particularly important because it is usually injected. Only a small minority of workers in the sex industry used a variety of other illegal mood modifying substances. Nonetheless, these rates tended to be higher than those observed in the general population.

Almost one quarter of the women had used injecting drugs. Compared with other workers, street workers, and those in the industry longer and from an earlier age, were more likely to report having used injecting drugs. Overall, our data suggested that, of the minority of workers who use injecting drugs, most act on an awareness of the risks involved. However, in isolated cases, workers may engage in high risk drug-taking practices.

Our study indicates that it is overly simplistic to assume that either drug use leads to prostitution or that involvement in prostitution leads to drug use. Women themselves suggest that their use of drugs is related to a number of factors including the social nature of their work, the occupational use of stimulants, coping mechanisms for difficult and stigmatised work, and an environment where drugs and 'instant cash' may be readily available.

7 Sexual and reproductive health

Considerable attention has been paid in recent years to the question of how adequately health services meet women's health needs. Yew and Need (1988), for example, highlighted several criticisms that have been raised including: issues of gender bias in health care decision making and delivery; a focus on treatment and abnormality rather than a recognition that women require services which address normal physiological functions, such as reproductive health; and a failure to consider the range of sociological factors that may contribute to health inequities affecting women.

Such issues are even more salient for women who work in the sex industry. As well as sharing the health needs and service deficiencies of women in the general population, their exposure to a range of health risks deriving directly from their work, means that they have additional needs, particularly in relation to sexual health. The stigma attached to sex work, and indeed its illegality, also have important implications for health service use.

In this chapter, we examine the health of female sex workers in terms of their reported level of health service usage. An overview is provided of patterns of health service utilisation, with particular attention to testing for STDs and HIV/AIDS. We also present a broad estimate of the (self-reported) prevalence of various STDs and provide information on reproductive health.

Health service use

Almost all (97 per cent) of the female sex workers surveyed had used some form of health service during the 12 months preceding the interview. Of a range of services, general practitioners appeared to be the main health care providers for this group of sex workers who presented mainly with general health concerns and for STD screening. As Table 7.1 shows, the majority of workers had consulted a general practitioner for general health reasons (73 per cent) or for STD checking

(65 per cent) during the last year. Very few women had used other specialised services such as STD clinics or family planning services. Interestingly, relatively few women reported having used medical services for reasons related to contraception.

Table 7.1
Health service usage by 200 female sex workers in the year preceding the interview

	General Health %	STD Checks %	Contraception %	Family/child health %	Drug/alcohol treatment %
General practitioner	73	65	4	4	1
Public STD clinic	2	14	0	0	0
Hospital outpatient department (STDs)	3	7	0	0	0
Private STD clinic	1	6	1	0	0
Drug clinic	0	0	0	0	4
Hospital outpatient department (not STDs)	2	1	0	1	1
Family Planning Centre	0	1	1	1	0
AIDS Medical Unit	0	1	0	0	0

There was a trend towards lower usage of health care services by younger workers ($p = 0.05$) but, overall, worker characteristics, including type of work, were not associated with use of health services during the previous year.

Level of satisfaction with health services

The majority of female sex workers (84 per cent) reported being satisfied with the sexual health services available to them at the time of the study. Only 10 per cent expressed dissatisfaction with available services and a further 6 per cent were noncommittal. Responses to an open-ended question by the 19 women who were not satisfied with available health services centred around the need for more STD clinics. Others indicated they would welcome improvements in the attitudes of medical staff. A small minority of women (6 per cent) claimed to have been refused services because they worked in the sex industry.

The high level of satisfaction with health services needs to be interpreted in the context of the general finding in the literature that most people, when surveyed, report being satisfied with their care (Pascoe, 1983). Level of satisfaction is only a gross indicator of the extent to which health services meet the needs of sex workers and a more accurate picture would require a more detailed evaluation.

The qualitative interviews revealed a perception among some sex workers that a certain degree of stigma is attached to attendance at STD clinics. The two workers in Inset 7.1 provided some insight into why sex workers may prefer to consult general practitioners rather than STD clinics. Some doctors appear to cater to the specific needs of sex workers and, as such, become known as 'the working girls' doctors'. General practitioners tended to be perceived as offering a service that was more personalised and broader in its health focus when compared with the narrower focus of STD clinics.

Inset 7.1

'... there are a few doctors in Brisbane who are known as the working girls' doctors. They were non-judgmental and had pathology out the back so you got your results within a couple of days ... I think that a lot of people, when they walk through the door of an STD clinic, feel like the whole world is outside watching them, thinking they have got some dirty disease. If it could be discreet, if there was some way to lose the stigma so that people can be proud of going for checkups rather than feel guilty and shameful. Just to lift the whole image of the STD clinic, maybe call it something else. The services I have had there have been fantastic. They have been very nice, the waiting time has been absolutely minimal and they were very thorough.'

(INTERVIEW 1)

What medical services do you use?
I go to my own private doctor. He's very good, he's very thorough and he's also not only concerned with your health, but he's also concerned with just how you're doing generally ... I just prefer my own doctor. Sure, it costs me, but [at a clinic] you never know which doctor you're going to see and it's always kind of awkward ... when you're having a different doctor every time you go for a check. I feel comfortable with my doctor doing my checks.

(INTERVIEW 5)

Other workers, however, had a clear preference for STD clinics. As illustrated in Inset 7.2, the perceived advantages of these services included their relative anonymity, their comprehensive approach to STD testing, and the one-stop nature of the service.

Inset 7.2

> *Where do you go for your tests?*
> STD clinics ... I just tell them some story, that I just found out that my boyfriend's been mucking around on me.
>
> **(INTERVIEW 6)**
>
> 'Oh, the clinic, most definitely. They're far more confidential ... some go to GPs, but they're not thorough ... they may take one or two tests but that's it. When you go to the clinic, you can get all sorts of small tests done and also you can wait for your results as well.'
>
> **(INTERVIEW 10)**

STD testing

At the time the study was conducted, only about one in five (21 per cent) workers were required by their employers to provide a medical certificate in order to work. Among those 40 women there was considerable variation in the frequency with which they were required to produce a medical certificate. In most cases, health clearances were necessary every one to three months (73 per cent), but in a small number of cases women were required to obtain a medical certificate as often as weekly (15 per cent) or fortnightly (13 per cent).

Since only a minority of workers were required to have regular medical checks, it was usually up to the individual worker to decide how often STD screening was sought. Figure 7.1 shows the frequency with which workers reported having STD checks. While it is important to keep in mind the self-report nature of these data, it appeared that a majority of workers had STD checks at intervals of between one and three months. Some 20 per cent of women had checks on a less regular basis including 3 per cent who stated that they did not have STD checks at all. These six women indicated that, for various reasons, they thought they were unnecessary.

Women who had been working in Queensland five years ago were also asked if the frequency with which they had STD checks had changed. This was of some interest given the changes that had occurred during this period in terms of both the socio-political climate surrounding the sex industry and the increased attention given to sexual health issues as a result of the advent of AIDS. Of the 30 women who answered this question, responses were evenly divided: 40 per cent claimed to have STD checks less often now but 60 per cent stated that they had not reduced the frequency of such checks. Notably, all 12 women who reported a reduction in frequency of STD checking stated that this was because they used condoms all the time.

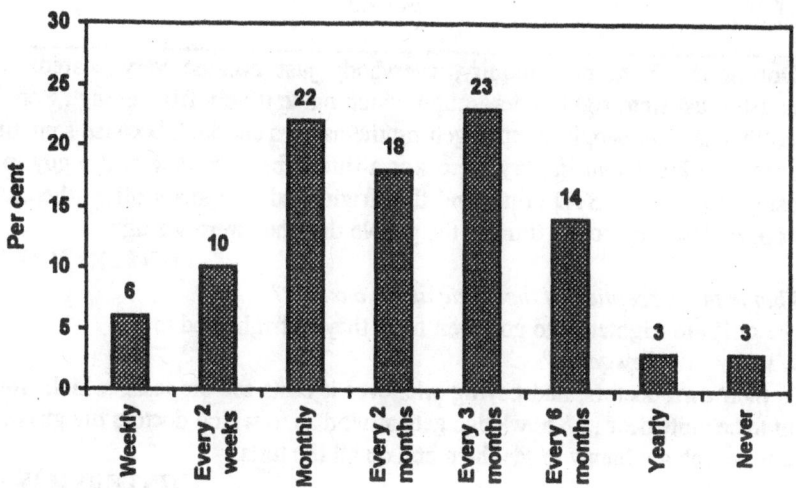

Figure 7.1 Frequency with which 194 female sex workers attended for STD check-ups

This small group of women who were working five years ago indicated that their source of health care for STD checks had not varied over time. Five years ago, as now, private doctors (60 per cent) and STD clinics (47 per cent) were most often consulted. However, the qualitative data were not altogether consistent with this. Some workers, such as those in Inset 7.3, were emphatic in stating that since the Fitzgerald Inquiry, they had observed among workers a high level of apprehension regarding STD clinic attendance and that this may have led to higher rates of general practice consultations.

Inset 7.3

> 'During the Fitzgerald Inquiry, everybody just became very scared. The industry just went right underground which made it very frightening ... on the health side of it, people stopped getting themselves checked, because sometime during the Fitzgerald Inquiry there was a threat, because they sent a guy in to inspect files at the STD clinic and that frightened everybody off ... the clinic dropped down to about a third of the people that they were seeing.'
> (INTERVIEW 10)
>
> *What is the perception of the clinic at the moment?*
> The girls are frightened to go. Even now, they're frightened to go.
> *So where are they going?*
> To their own doctors, and paying whatever it costs for the tests, which works out to be quite dear ... Knowledge gets around as to which doctors the girls can go to, which are happy to see them and do all the tests.
> (INTERVIEW 11)

As shown in Table 7.2, the frequency with which workers reported having STD checks varied considerably depending on the type of work in which they were engaged. Specifically, street workers appeared less likely than other workers to have regular STD checks ($p < 0.001$).

Table 7.2
Frequency of STD check-ups by type of work

	Brothel (N=30)	Parlour Escort (N=45)	Escort Agency (N=56)	Street (N=11)	Private (N=52)
	%	%	%	%	%
At least monthly	43	31	46	18	35
Every 2 to 3 months	37	42	41	18	46
Once or twice a year	13	27	9	18	19
Never	7	0	4	45	0

Other variables such as the worker's present age, the age at which she had entered the industry, and the length of time in the industry were not associated with the frequency of STD checks.

HIV/AIDS testing

Our data suggested that HIV/AIDS testing was widespread among female sex workers. Almost all the workers in the sample (96 per cent) reported having been tested for HIV/AIDS at some time. As noted earlier, none of the workers reported being HIV positive. However, one woman did report having received a positive test result on one occasion.

The reliance of female sex workers on general practitioners for their health care needs is again illustrated in Table 7.3 which shows that two thirds of the women had consulted a doctor for HIV/AIDS testing. In comparison, just over one quarter of the women had attended an STD clinic for this purpose. Relatively few women had used any other health services for such tests.

Wide variation existed in terms of the reported frequency of HIV/AIDS testing but, most often, workers reported being tested for HIV/AIDS every three to six months (Figure 7.2). Some (28 per cent) reported having been tested more frequently but, at the other extreme were a minority of women who were tested only every one or two years (8 per cent) or who did not have regular HIV/AIDS tests at all (5 per cent). Presumably, in this latter group, some would be tested if they thought they had been exposed to the HIV virus.

Table 7.3
**Source of HIV/AIDS testing for 191 female sex workers
(multiple responses possible)**

	%
General Practitioner	66
STD Clinic	27
Hospital	9
Family Planning	2
SQWISI	2
Other	4

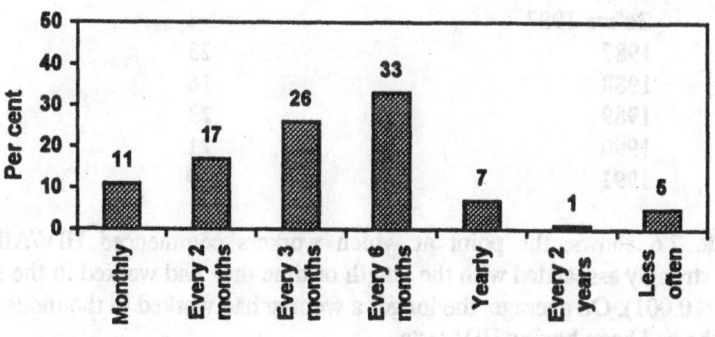

Figure 7.2 Frequency of HIV testing among 189 female sex workers

The data shown in Table 7.4 concern patterns of HIV testing according to type of work. When compared with data for STD checking (see Table 7.2), there was some suggestion that street workers were more likely to have HIV/AIDS testing than STD checks. Patterns of HIV testing were not associated with other worker characteristics such as current age, age at entry to the industry or length of time in the sex industry.

Table 7.5 shows when the women first began having regular HIV/AIDS tests. Particularly striking is the sharp increase in the proportion of women who began testing around 1987. This is most likely accounted for by the 'Grim Reaper' national HIV public awareness campaign which was introduced in Australia at this time.

Table 7.4
Frequency of HIV testing by type of work

	Brothel (N=30)	Parlour Escort (N=45)	Escort Agency (N=56)	Street (N=11)	Private (N=52)
	%	%	%	%	%
Every 1 to 2 months	23	28	36	0	24
Every 3 to 6 months	58	55	47	64	64
Every 1 to 2 years	10	11	4	18	6
Less often or never	10	6	13	18	6

Table 7.5
Year in which 189 female sex workers commenced HIV/AIDS testing

	%
Before 1987	8
1987	23
1988	16
1989	23
1990	21
1991	9

As Table 7.6 shows, the point at which workers commenced HIV/AIDS testing was strongly associated with the length of time they had worked in the sex industry ($p < 0.001$). On average, the longer a woman had worked in the industry, the longer she had been having HIV tests.

Table 7.6
Commencement of regular HIV/AIDS testing by length of time in the sex industry

	< 2 years (N=59) %	2-9 years (N=100) %	10+ years (N=29) %
Before 1987	5	3	34
Between 1987-1989	37	74	66
Between 1990-1991	58	23	0

Sexual health

Table 7.7 presents data regarding rates of STDs among sex workers in the study. These rates reflect the workers' own reports of diagnosed conditions only. Some workers may have been unaware that they had a particular STD and for this reason the figures presented are likely to be conservative estimates of actual rates.

Table 7.7
Self-reported rates of STDs among 200 female sex workers

	% Ever diagnosed		% Recently diagnosed *
	Once	>Once	(Within last 2 years)
Chlamydia	13	15	75
Thrush	10	32	88
Trichomoniasis	1	3	50
Gonorrhoea (anal)	0	0	--
Gonorrhoea (oral)	<1	0	0
Gonorrhoea (vaginal)	3	2	25
Herpes (anal)	0	0	--
Herpes (oral)	<1	7	87
Herpes (vaginal)	2	5	71
Warts (anal)	0	0	--
Warts (vaginal)	2	1	33
Syphilis (anal)	0	0	--
Syphilis (vaginal)	0	0	--
Crabs/lice	9	21	82
Cervical cancer	<1	0	0
Pre-cancer	1	0	<1

* Per cent of those ever diagnosed

The most prevalent STDs, appeared to be thrush (42 per cent), crabs or lice (30 per cent), and chlamydia (28 per cent). These generally tended to be recurrent conditions. In the case of thrush, for instance, 32 per cent of women reported having been diagnosed on more than one occasion, while only 10 per cent reported a single episode. Similarly, 21 per cent reported multiple episodes of crabs/lice compared with 9 per cent diagnosed once. Similar numbers of women had been diagnosed with chlamydia on one (13 per cent) or more than one (15 per cent) occasion. Most of the women who had ever been diagnosed with these STDs had experienced at least one occurrence of the condition within the last two years.

Oral and vaginal herpes, vaginal gonorrhoea, trichomoniasis, and vaginal warts, while much less common, had been diagnosed in 3 to 8 per cent of the sex workers. Again, the women affected had often experienced these as recurrent conditions, particularly in the case of herpes. Herpes also tended to have been experienced more recently by the affected women. Only isolated cases of cervical cancer, pre-cancer, and oral gonorrhoea were reported. None of the women reported ever having had vaginal syphilis or any anal STDs.

Rates of the more commonly reported STDs (chlamydia, thrush, and crabs or lice) did not tend to vary according to worker characteristics. However, it was difficult to make meaningful comparisons because these characteristics also tended to be associated with STD checking thus reducing the rates of diagnosed conditions in some groups.

About two thirds (64 per cent) of the women who reported STDs attributed these conditions to work in the sex industry. The remaining women indicated that they had contracted the STD in their private life. This again highlights the importance of focusing not only on risks inherent in the sex industry, but also on personal circumstances.

The data suggested that untreated symptoms were relatively uncommon among the women in the sample. Only about 10 per cent reported having delayed medical treatment for a possible STD symptom, such as a discharge or rash, during the preceding year. Of these 19 workers who had delayed seeking medical attention, itchiness was by far the most common symptom (95 per cent). Discharge (16 per cent), pain when urinating (16 per cent), rash (16 per cent) or wart-like bumps (5 per cent) had also been ignored by a smaller number of women. Most (68 per cent) of these women had simply thought the symptom not serious enough to warrant treatment. Only one woman had ignored her symptoms because she had felt too embarrassed to seek treatment. In 9 of the 19 untreated cases, the symptoms remitted spontaneously while 8 women did eventually see a doctor. The other two women stated that they had treated the symptoms themselves.

Table 7.8 shows the proportion of women who reported having ever had a positive hepatitis result. Additionally, 2 per cent of the women did not know if they had ever tested positive.

Table 7.8
Self-reported prevalence of hepatitis among 195 female sex workers

	%
Hepatitis A	2
Hepatitis B	6
Hepatitis C	6

Reproductive health

Most of the women (92 per cent) reported having had a pap smear on at least one occasion. A small number of women (6 per cent) did not know whether they had ever had this test and a further 2 per cent had not been tested. Women who had never had a pap smear, or who were unsure, more often were aged under 20 at the time of the interview ($p = 0.02$) and had started in the sex industry before the age of 20 ($p = 0.04$). Consistent with this, street workers and, to a lesser extent, massage parlour or brothel workers, were significantly less likely to report having had a pap smear ($p = 0.001$).

Women who reported having had a pap smear, tended to have the test on a regular basis (Table 7.9). The majority (78 per cent) reported attending for a pap smear once or twice a year and a further 21 per cent stated that they were tested more regularly.

Table 7.9
Frequency of pap smear testing for 182 female sex workers ever tested

	%
Monthly	6
Every two months	5
Every three or four months	10
Every six months	50
Yearly	28
Every two years	1

The contraceptive pill was the most frequently used form of birth control (Table 7.10). However, it was notable that about one third of the women reported that they did not use any form of contraception.

Table 7.10
Type of contraception used by 196 female sex workers

	%
Contraceptive pill	51
Condoms only	9
Diaphragm	6
Other	1
None	34

The observation that a relatively large number of women did not use birth control needs to be treated tentatively. Some women may have misunderstood the question which specifically asked for methods of contraception. Condoms may be used more widely than Table 7.10 would suggest but are viewed primarily as a method of reducing the risk of STDs as in the case of the worker in Inset 7.4.

Inset 7.4

> *Are you using contraception apart from condoms?*
> No.
> *Do you prefer to use condoms or since you are using them anyway you don't think it's necessary?*
> No, because I am using them anyway, I just don't bother, plus I possibly wouldn't be able to fall pregnant anyway.
> **(INTERVIEW 10)**

The form of contraception used by sex workers in the study varied markedly according to their type of work (Table 7.11). It was largely street workers who contributed to this variation in that the majority of street workers who responded to this question reported not using any form of contraception ($p < 0.01$). Birth control methods did not differ according to the age of workers, the age at which they had been working or the length of time they had been working in the sex industry.

Table 7.11
Form of contraception by type of work

	Brothel (N=30)	Parlour Escort (N=46)	Escort Agency (N=57)	Street (N=11)	Private (N=52)
	%	%	%	%	%
Pill	40	59	58	18	50
Other	20	24	5	9	15
None	40	17	37	73	35

Work-related pregnancies

About 10 per cent of the workers reported that they had become pregnant as a result of work on at least one occasion (Table 7.12). A small number of women (3 per cent), including the worker in Inset 7.5, reported more than one work-related pregnancy.

Table 7.12
Number of times 198 female sex workers had become pregnant through work

	%
Never	90
Once	7
Twice	2
Three times	1

Inset 7.5

> *How many pregnancies have you had?*
> Two. They're both parlour babies.
> **(INTERVIEW 12)**

As Table 7.13 shows, the likelihood of a work-related pregnancy increased with the length of time a woman had spent in the sex industry ($p < 0.001$). In all, almost one third of the 29 women who had worked in the sex industry for 10 years or more had become pregnant as a result of their work.

Table 7.13
Number of times pregnant through work by length of time in sex industry

	< 2 years (N=62) %	2-9 years (N=106) %	10+ years (N=29) %
None	98	91	69
One or more	2	9	31

Neither the worker's present age nor the age at which she had started in the industry were significantly associated with the likelihood of a work-related pregnancy. While this was also the case for type of work, it is notable that the small group of street workers appeared to account for a disproportionate number of work-related pregnancies (Table 7.14).

Table 7.14
Number of times pregnant through work by type of work

	Brothel (N=30) %	Parlour Escort (N=48) %	Escort Agency (N=57) %	Street (N=11) %	Private (N=52) %
None	93	92	95	73	85
One or more	7	8	5	27	15

Summary

Almost all of the female sex workers in this study had consulted a medical service in the year preceding the interview and, overall, most seemed satisfied with the services available to them. Overwhelmingly, sex workers appeared to use mainstream health services, relying heavily on general practitioners for their two main forms of health care: general health needs and STD checks. HIV testing was also carried out by general practitioners in the majority of cases.

Most workers reported having STD checks on a regular basis and the majority had checks at least every three months. Similarly, almost all workers reported having been tested for HIV and the majority stated that they attended for such testing at least every six months. A sharp increase in the number of workers who began HIV testing appeared to have coincided with the introduction of an intensive national media campaign to heighten AIDS awareness. The majority of workers also had regular pap smear tests. Yet despite these relatively high rates of testing, a small group of women reported that they did not have regular checks.

The variable which most consistently distinguished this group was type of work, with street workers reporting lower rates of STD testing, pap smears and contraceptive usage.

The contraceptive pill was the single most commonly reported form of birth control but some women reported using no form of contraception. Around 10 per cent of workers reported that they had become pregnant as a result of work.

The most prevalent STDs in the sample were chlamydia, thrush and crabs/lice each of which had been diagnosed in around one third of the women. Only isolated instances of other STDs were reported. These figures can be treated only as broad estimates, however, due to the self-report nature of the data and the possibility of undiagnosed cases.

8   Training and support needs

All workers in the sex industry potentially are exposed to a variety of health-related and other risks. While screening for STDs and HIV/AIDS is an essential component of sex worker health, these are secondary forms of prevention. Primary prevention requires workers to incorporate safe practices into all sexual encounters and other potential risk behaviours.

To protect and promote the health of sex workers, it is therefore essential that they have access to accurate information that is presented in a manner and form conducive to sustained behavioural change. Such educational efforts may assist sex workers to develop the skills necessary to reduce health-related risks and to improve their general level of well-being. One model that may be particularly effective involves peer-based education. Fisher (1988) notes that two key principles underpin this model. First, to be effective, informational, educational and other supportive initiatives must be consistent with group values. Second, they should come from someone who is actually a member of the particular peer group.

This section considers how sex workers acquire relevant knowledge and the extent to which they are supported in meeting a variety of needs, including the decision to leave the industry. We pay particular attention to the role of SQWISI, a community-based organisation operated for and by workers in the sex industry.

Training for work in the sex industry

Despite the numerous and particularly serious 'occupational hazards' faced by workers in the sex industry, one gains the impression that many female workers enter the industry with little real knowledge of many of these hazards or how to reduce them. In few other industries is it likely that workers would be expected to deal with workplace hazards in such an *ad hoc* manner. However, training, open discussion and information exchange about HIV transmission and risk reduction are considerably less likely to take place given the covert context in which the sex industry operates.

The vast majority (92 per cent) of female workers in this study were in favour of a training period for new sex workers prior to commencing work in the industry. Almost all workers who thought training was needed endorsed a number of key areas, including the proper use of condoms, STD checking, and client management (Table 8.1).

Table 8.1
Training areas suggested by 185 female sex workers
(multiple responses possible)

	%
How to use condoms	100
How to do STD checks	99
Managing violent or difficult clients	95
Sexual services	95
Negotiating with clients	92
Other	10

The women most often viewed former sex workers as the most appropriate providers of training for new workers (Table 8.2). A sex worker support group such as SQWISI was the next most frequent response. It is notable that informal training by other workers in the sex industry was not usually considered an appropriate source of training. However, as shown earlier, this informal apprenticeship type training tended to prevail in the industry at the time of the survey. It is also notable that only about one in five women nominated health professionals (doctors or STD clinic staff) as the most appropriate sources of training for sex workers.

Table 8.2
Appropriate sources of training as identified by 185 female sex workers
(multiple responses possible)

	%
Ex-workers	71
Support group (e.g. SQWISI)	35
STD clinic staff	23
Doctors	20
Management	18
Informally by other workers	10
Other	2

Both the quantitative and qualitative data demonstrated that training by those who have first hand knowledge of the issues faced by workers in the industry would be most acceptable to workers. In this respect, the worker in Inset 8.1 expressed the views of many in the study. She also indicated the need to address a number of issues, including self-esteem and financial planning, in addition to safe sex.

Inset 8.1

Do you think some kind of training is important?
Oh certainly. I think there should be old retired madams or old ex-workers giving them all the ground rules, telling them how to check a man out, showing them the picture book so they really know what they are dealing with and helping them with their self-esteem in the first place so that they can be assertive in things like insisting on condoms or saying no to things they don't want to do. Assertiveness training, self-esteem, financial training so they don't blow all their money.

(INTERVIEW 1)

The situation that existed with regard to skills training at the time the survey was undertaken is explored further in Inset 8.2. It was evident that some workers had an extremely limited knowledge of issues such as STD checking. However, in some establishments, informal but fairly comprehensive training may be provided to all workers. Thus, some women simply enter the industry and 'learn as they go', possibly with input from other workers. Others are fortunate to be given more thorough training because this is their employer's policy. Legislative changes to the sex industry in Queensland are likely to have produced a situation where, at the present time, there exist even fewer opportunities for this workplace training.

Inset 8.2

'I worked on the coast for a while and some of the girls haven't got any idea what they're doing. They don't know how to check their clients, they don't know anything, and a lot of them haven't even been checked up for a couple of months.'

(INTERVIEW 9)

Did you try to train your staff in prevention?
Always.
And do the girls help each other?
Yes. If I wasn't there and somebody new was put on, the next girl in charge sat her down, spent an hour or two, went through everything, gave her the brochures, what to look for.

(INTERVIEW 11)

Issues of concern to sex workers

To gain an indication of the areas of most concern to sex workers, those in the study were asked to rank, in order of importance, issues that may lead them to seek information or advice. As Table 8.3 shows, health-related issues emerged as being of primary importance.

Table 8.3
Rankings of issues in order of importance by 185 female sex workers

	Rank 1 %	Rank 2 %	Rank 3 %
Health	62	18	9
Financial	21	32	17
Legal	8	17	28
Personal/social	4	15	18
Alternative employment/education	3	4	3
Tax	2	12	21
Alcohol and drug service	1	1	2

Almost two thirds of the workers cited health as the main issue for which they would seek assistance or advice and the large majority rated it as one of their three highest priorities. Financial issues were of next importance, followed by legal and tax-related concerns. Interestingly, relatively few female sex workers indicated that they would be likely to seek advice on personal or social matters. Even fewer indicated a need for advisory services about alcohol or drugs or alternative sources of employment or education. Whether this pattern of response reflects a low level of need among sex workers or a perceived lack of avenues for obtaining such assistance even if required, was not clear from the data.

Preferred sources of information

Table 8.4 provides data on sex workers' preferred sources of information about sexual health issues. SQWISI was rated the best source of information on STDs and HIV/AIDS by just over half the workers, highlighting the importance of the organisation as a source of relevant information. Consistent with the patterns of health service utilisation presented earlier, doctors and STD clinics were also favoured by some workers.

Table 8.4
Preferred sources of information on STDs and HIV/AIDS for 192 female sex workers (multiple responses possible)

	%
SQWISI	55
Doctor	41
STD clinic	35
Queensland AIDS Council	9
Book	8
Other workers/friends	7
Other	7

Two other sources of information were referred to by workers in Inset 8.3. These were popular magazines and word of mouth. As noted elsewhere, much information appeared to be disseminated informally by word of mouth. However, as the first respondent in Inset 8.3 pointed out, this could have adverse consequences if workers acquired and acted on misinformation. It is also likely that not all sex workers would be part of the informal network, with some working instead in relative isolation.

Inset 8.3

Where did you used to get your information when you were working?
I did visit the STD clinic on a regular basis and I also had a private doctor that I went to. A lot of information is spread by word of mouth, like there is an outbreak of chlamydia or whatever. They talk among themselves, but there are a lot of untruths in any information being passed on. They think they know it all because so and so down the road told them. The information they are getting is not accurate.

(INTERVIEW 1)

'... well there's *Cleo* and *Cosmopolitan*, they often have articles ... the clinic in town or places like [SQWISI] where you can pick up information ...'

(INTERVIEW 4)

Overall, most workers (85 per cent) considered the information available to them about STDs and HIV to be good or excellent. While a minority (14 per cent) indicated that more such information needed to be made available, all workers appeared to have access to at least some information.

SQWISI appeared to have a high profile in that almost all workers (95 per cent) had heard of the organisation. While this needs to be interpreted in terms of the fact that many study participants were recruited through SQWISI, it is also likely to reflect the high level of outreach undertaken by the organisation. At the time of the study, much publicity about the group appeared to have occurred informally by word of mouth. As Table 8.5 shows, workers had most often heard about the group through a friend.

Table 8.5
How 187 female sex workers first heard of SQWISI

	%
From a friend	58
From management	34
From STD clinic	2
From drug clinic	1
Other	4

Most of the other workers had heard about SQWISI from management. Only in isolated cases had workers heard about the group from health professionals such as those consulted at STD clinics. This of course may simply reflect the fact that most sex workers were already aware of SQWISI, rather than indicate limited referral by health care workers.

Table 8.6 examines the level of worker involvement with SQWISI at the time the study was carried out. Just over half the workers reported that they were members of SQWISI and/or received the group's regular publication, *RESPECT* (or the then *Hookers' Herald*). However, few women appeared to have direct contact with SQWISI as either active participants in the group or as recipients of services offered by the group.

Table 8.6
Level of contact with SQWISI for 193 female sex workers
(multiple responses possible)

	%
Member	57
Receive publication (*RESPECT*)	53
Know members who keep informed	33
Have attended workshops	10
Have sought help with a specific problem	7
Volunteer	1

Despite this, almost all women (97 per cent) stated that they were happy with the services it provided, suggesting that SQWISI addressed the needs of many workers in the industry. The worker in Inset 8.4 expressed the view of many in the study, that the organisation is both much needed and valued.

Inset 8.4

> 'I haven't had a great deal to do with [SQWISI] but they are a good department to have, because at least it gives the girls somewhere to go if they have problems or if they need help with work, things like that. Yes, I think it's a needed department.'
>
> (INTERVIEW 10)

As in the case of other health services, the above observation should be viewed in the context of the more general finding that clients typically express very high levels of satisfaction with particular health care agencies. More specific questioning about the various functions of the group would be needed to obtain a more detailed evaluation of SQWISI services. While this was beyond the scope of the current study, some women did offer suggestions as to how services could be enhanced. These covered a number of issues, but most commonly cited were: greater regional contact for workers in regional areas; increased worker involvement; and more personal contact with workers.

Worker support programs

Many workers favoured the introduction of special programs to assist those who wished to leave the sex industry. However, the demand for such services would not appear to be overwhelming. While 57 per cent of the workers thought special programs should exist, about one third (32 per cent) did not see such programs as necessary and a further 10 per cent did not know if they were needed. Even fewer women (28 per cent) said they would be interested in participating in such a program if it did exist. Again, it is not clear whether this reflects an actual low-need situation or a certain scepticism about the value of such programs. It is clear, however, that any effort to design a program to assist and support workers in the transition from sex work to more conventional forms of employment would need to involve close liaison with a wide range of workers to ensure that it was both appropriate and acceptable.

Many workers nominated issues that would need to be addressed if support was to be provided for women who wished to leave the industry (Table 8.7). Personal counselling, access to training courses and study grants, and drug and alcohol counselling were most often mentioned.

The qualitative data offered valuable insights into the difficulties faced by women leaving the industry. One theme that emerged repeatedly throughout the interviews was that, despite the potentially lucrative nature of sex work, many workers had limited financial management skills and were often left with nothing even after many years in the industry (Inset 8.5).

Table 8.7
Programs suggested by 133 female sex workers to help workers leave the industry (multiple responses possible)

	%
Personal counselling	82
Access to training courses	74
Drug and alcohol counselling or treatment	73
Access to special study grants	56
Child care facilities	47
Financial help	44
Accommodation	24
Assistance with removal costs	19

Inset 8.5

> '... there are a lot of ladies still in the industry for getting on 20 years, you know, and they're getting in their early 40s or whatever and they still have absolutely nothing to show and I think that's really sad, you know ... I mean, I know at 40 I still don't want to be in this industry and have absolutely nothing ...'
>
> (INTERVIEW 6)
>
> 'Rich one day, poor the next ... I've seen it time and time again. All the money they earn is always in cash ... most of the women in the industry can't budget. I was lucky, I was older.'
>
> (INTERVIEW 14)

This of course is not always the case as was illustrated by the workers in Inset 8.6 who had purposefully saved money for a set goal. Nonetheless, workers who succeed in accumulating material resources may well be the exceptions to the general case and, for many, the long term financial outlook may be far from secure.

The second issue raised during interviews involved the barriers to finding alternative forms of employment when workers decided to leave the industry. This situation, which was particularly salient for older women who had been in the industry for some time, was described by the worker in Inset 8.7. Women are usually unable to disclose to potential employers the nature of their previous work and their work experience cannot readily be transferred to other employment settings. Without some form of retraining program, the viable employment options for former sex workers may be very limited.

Inset 8.6

'... When I leave the industry, I want to walk out with my house, maybe have a year to be a full-time mum again and then go back into the workforce ... with the workers the money comes in so easy and you don't think of the next day. Maybe it might be quiet ... so you think, "Oh well, I've got $400 today, I'm going to go out and buy that leather jacket I've seen ... I'll get another job before the night's out, or tomorrow I'll get another anyway". It's a lifestyle but there's always the quiet days and you think, "Oh, shit I haven't got enough money for the rent". It would be very easy to spend every cent you earned, I could.'

(INTERVIEW 17)

How do you spend the money?
In the bank mostly. I'm trying to buy a house so most of it is going in the bank.

(INTERVIEW 19)

Inset 8.7

Do you think there should be some kind of retraining for girls who want to get out of the parlours?
Yes. I don't know how it would work but definitely. I've got a lot of personal friends who would love to get out of the parlour. I mean, especially getting around my age, but they don't know what to do. How can you go and apply for a job and explain what you've done for the last ten years to anybody? You've got nothing to back up. You can't walk into a straight job and say 'Look, I've been working as a prostitute for the last ten years' and they give you the job, so it's very hard to get out of the parlour situation. The most that can happen is you decide not to work and you get a job as a receptionist.

(INTERVIEW 13)

Sex workers as client educators

Much emphasis so far has been placed on the need to ensure that sex workers are aware of strategies such as safe sex behaviours to minimise the risk of transmission of HIV/AIDS and other STDs. Equally important, however, is the need to educate clients of sex workers regarding the dangers of engaging in high risk sexual activities. This is underlined by data presented earlier, regarding the frequency with which clients ask for non-condom sex. As Perkins, Lovejoy and Jacobsen (1996) point out, there is a need to develop among male clients a 'health consciousness' in relation to safe sex so that sex workers do not have to go into 'daily battle' with clients.

While sex workers as a group are difficult to access, targeting the clients of sex workers is likely to be even more problematic. Apart from mounting widespread campaigns which target the whole population, it may be that the most effective method of providing information to clients is to do so at the time of their encounters with sex workers.

More than three quarters of the female workers in this study (81 per cent) believed they offered a source of information and education for their clients about STD and HIV/AIDS prevention. As shown in Table 8.8, many workers indicated that they would welcome access to written material for distribution to their clients. A smaller number of workers also favoured some form of government-run education program to assist them to develop appropriate skills in passing on information to clients.

Table 8.8
Resources suggested by 191 female sex workers to educate clients
(multiple responses possible)

	%
Written material for clients	53
Client education programs run by the government	38
Special training about STDs	26
Client education programs run by SQWISI	9
Other	2

Inset 8.8 offers a qualitative perspective on the educative role of sex workers in relation to their clients and again highlights an expressed need for the availability of appropriate printed information for clients. The potentially important role of the sex worker in educating clients about sexual health is perhaps best summed up by the second respondent who considers workers to be in the 'front line' with respect to the prevention of STDs.

While many sex workers are likely to provide information verbally, some appear to make available to clients leaflets such as those published by health departments. As the first respondent in Inset 8.8 pointed out, the back-up of printed information from an authoritative source is likely to have most impact. Some clients may view the sex worker as 'just a hooker' and an unlikely source of reliable information. However, the second respondent in Inset 8.8 indicated that other clients were likely to be receptive to information they received through their encounters with sex workers.

Inset 8.8

> 'When I was having problems with a client not wanting to wear a condom I would explain to him the reasons why and the feeling I'd get back from him would be "what would you know, you're just a hooker". So I kept a supply of Health Department pamphlets backing up what I had to say and I highlighted parts of them.'
>
> (INTERVIEW 1)
>
> 'The clients are slowly becoming more and more educated through the girls. I myself have experienced that, you know, I've had clients say to me "I didn't know that" and I really feel that the clients in general are becoming more aware of exactly what the situation is now, and we as workers in the industry are in the front line, so to speak, in the war against sexually transmitted diseases ... slowly more and more clients are actually becoming aware of the dangers involved through contact with the girls, and I think that's good. I think that the more education material and resources that are available for workers, the more there is the better.'
>
> (INTERVIEW 5)

Summary

This chapter has outlined the nature and availability of various forms of information, training, and support relevant to workers in the sex industry. In doing so, it has pointed to a number of initiatives that could be considered as part of a comprehensive effort to protect and improve the health of women who are consistently exposed to high-risk situations. Clear support exists for ensuring that workers have access to training, in such areas as condom usage and client management, at an early stage. Scope also exists for making available to workers a variety of support services that would include training in financial management and retraining opportunities to assist workers who wish to leave the industry.

The data underline the importance of close liaison with sex workers before any programs are developed. Training or other services are unlikely to be acceptable to sex workers unless they are conducted by individuals who have first hand experience in the sex industry. At the time of the study, SQWISI appeared to have gone some way to providing a valued source of information and support as well as a forum for sex workers. Given the underground nature of the sex industry, it is not surprising that word of mouth seems to be a powerful means of information dissemination. While this type of networking can be viewed as a positive feature of the sex industry, the challenge is to ensure that the information which reaches sex workers is accurate. Finally, it would be a mistake to exclude clients from educational initiatives directed towards the sex industry. Workers themselves seem to offer a valuable opportunity to transmit health messages to clients who otherwise may be very difficult to reach.

9 Contact with the police and legal system

In this chapter we are concerned with the degree and nature of contact between sex workers and the police force. This contact is considered from two perspectives. First, it might be expected that workers as a group have a relatively high level of contact with the police and legal system because they regularly violate the law. At the same time, there is reason to suspect that sex workers may have a relatively high level of contact with the police force because the nature of their work puts them at particular risk for being the victims of crime.

Relationship between workers and police

Curiously, relatively few female workers (12 per cent) reported ever having been charged with any of a range of offences related to sex work. This suggests that police have rarely charged sex workers. This study may also have accessed a wider range of workers than many other studies which often rely on 'captive' populations such as those in treatment or already in prison for example. Indeed, as Table 9.1 shows, the majority of women reported having little or no involvement with the police during the last twelve months. Among those who had been involved with the police, there was considerable diversity in terms of how those encounters were perceived.

Table 9.1
Relationship between 199 female sex workers and police in last year

	%
No involvement	61
Excellent, good or average	28
Not so good or poor	11

Reporting of offences

Of considerable importance in terms of the wellbeing of sex workers is the question of whether they would report offences against them to police if the need arose. Anecdotally, it has been suggested that there exists a certain reluctance on the part of sex industry workers to become involved with police, even if the situation calls for it. We asked women to indicate whether they would report a range of offences (Table 9.2). The likelihood of reporting to police was remarkably similar for various crimes, including assault, rape and robbery. Moreover, this likelihood did not vary irrespective of whether the perpetrator was a client or personal partner.

Table 9.2
Likelihood of 199 female sex workers reporting offences to police

	Yes %	No %	Maybe %
Assault by a client	54	31	15
Rape by a client	58	30	12
Robbery by a client	54	32	13
Assault by non-paying partner	55	30	14
Rape by a non-paying partner	59	26	15
Robbery by non-paying partner	57	29	15

In all instances involving a client or non-paying partner, just over half the female workers were consistent in stating that they would report the offence to police. About one third of women said they would not report the crime to police. For all offences, a minority of women were uncertain whether or not they would report the crime.

Overall, one gains the impression of a reluctance among sex workers to report crimes to police. While this general conclusion needs to be interpreted in the context of high rates of unreported crime in the general community it is, nonetheless, of practical significance given the potentially high-risk situations some sex workers may encounter.

Reasons for not-reporting offences

Table 9.3 examines the reasons most often given by workers who stated they would not report one or more of the above offences to police.

Table 9.3
Reasons given by 98 female sex workers for not reporting offences
(multiple responses possible)

	%
I don't want to bring myself to police attention	47
The police would not take it seriously	35
The police might charge me with a prostitution offence	29
I'd be in more trouble with my client/partner	17
Police want me for something else	1
Other	6

Clearly, many workers simply did not want to bring themselves to the attention of police. While others preferred to avoid the possibility of being charged with a prostitution offence, very rarely were they attempting to escape other charges. More than one third of the women thought their complaint would not be taken seriously by the police while a smaller proportion of women thought that involving the police would worsen existing difficulties with a client or partner.

Inset 9.1 gives a qualitative perspective on sex workers' views about reporting offences to police. Here, we see that some sex workers perceived the police force as offering them little protection because of the nature of their work.

Inset 9.1

'It's been my experience that if a girl is raped, bashed, ripped off, robbed or anything like that in the past the police have not been any great protection, in fact they've been quite judgemental. The attitude that comes across is "What do you expect, you're a hooker. You know this kind of thing is going to happen to you". It's almost as though because they are doing one illegal thing, they lose all their other rights to legal access to the police upholding the law.'

(INTERVIEW 1)

Have you come across much rape or violence in the industry?
Quite a few of the lone girls have been attacked.
Are any of these incidents reported to the Police?
Never.

(INTERVIEW 10)

'To say that [sex workers] shouldn't receive protection is like saying that a bank teller shouldn't receive protection, you know, it's like saying he asked to be robbed because he was a bank teller.'

(INTERVIEW 4)

Rape and other violence in the sex industry

Almost one third (29 per cent) of the women in the study had been raped on at least one occasion, though it should be noted that this figure includes rapes that occurred outside the sex industry as well as prior to the worker entering the industry. Other qualitative data suggest that, prior to the Fitzgerald Inquiry, protection, and even retribution, was provided by syndicate owners if a worker was attacked. Overall, while the majority reported never having been raped, a small number of sex workers appeared to have been exposed to repeated incidents of rape by clients, or, less often, by a personal partner.

A similar number (30 per cent) of the female sex workers reported having been bashed on one or more occasions. Patterns of such physical assault were similar to those reported for rape. Most workers appeared to have avoided such violence but a small percentage had been involved in multiple incidents.

The issue of violence in the sex industry is one that is important and although our data suggest that such incidents are not commonplace, as we have noted, these events may be grossly under-reported to police. In interviews, some sex workers expressed reservations about approaching legal authorities with complaints about assault, apparently because they might suffer some form of retribution as a consequence and because, on occasion, their complaints had not been received with sympathy. In this study, workers were interviewed by a sympathetic interviewer and should have felt free to report rapes and assaults. It follows that, while the data are probably correct in indicating that assaults and rapes are not everyday occurrences, they nevertheless remain of great concern to workers in the industry and the gravity of some of these incidents is illustrated in Inset 9.2.

Inset 9.2

> 'I hadn't been very long in the business when a young man produced a rifle, said he had no money and threatened to shoot me ... My main concern was to get out of there alive. I have had two other clients pull knives on me in different situations and different places.'
>
> **(INTERVIEW 1)**
>
> *Have you ever been raped at work?*
> Yes.
> *On what occasions?*
> Twice on the street, once really badly bashed. I was pregnant at the time too ... and I was bashed and raped.
> *Were there other occasions too?*
> Yes, there was a couple where I ... well any other normal person would consider it rape I suppose except that I was in a position where I couldn't really scream rape but where I had asked it to stop and got slapped around a little bit and continued to ... that was on the street as well.
> *And did you report the incidents to the police?*
> No.
> *What did you do about it?*
> Nothing. I did nothing.
>
> **(INTERVIEW 12)**

Summary

Most workers reported little or no contact with police. Of the 39 per cent who did report police contact in the last 12 months, less than one third described their relationship with police as 'not so good' or 'poor'. Despite this, little over half the women stated that they would definitely report a serious crime (assault, rape or robbery) to the police. The three reasons most commonly given for this reluctance to approach the police were: not wanting to come to police attention; the belief that they would not be taken seriously; and the fear that they would be charged with a prostitution offence. In general, violence in the sex industry is a threat for workers, with almost one third stating that they had experienced physical or sexual assault.

10 Male sex workers

This chapter presents an overview of the sex industry in Queensland from a male worker perspective. Because our results were based on only 28 male workers who took part in the study, it was difficult to draw firm conclusions regarding this group. While they are likely to form a smaller group than female workers, male workers were probably under-represented because they are a more difficult to reach group. None of the massage parlours approached regarding the study employed male workers and, as our data indicated, a relatively large proportion of male sex workers appeared to work from the street. In the following discussion, we focus on a number of key issues to highlight some of the similarities and differences between the male and female workers who took part in the study. We consider worker characteristics and services offered, health-related issues including risk practices, substance use, and exposure to and reporting of sexual and other violent assaults.

Approach to sex work

In the broadest sense, male and female workers appeared to approach sex work in fairly similar ways. All but one of the male sex workers exchanged sex mainly for money but several also accepted drugs, alcohol, goods, services, food or shelter in payment for sex on occasions. Most male workers appeared to be motivated primarily by financial concerns, having entered the industry because they needed the money (68 per cent) and less often with a particular goal in mind (14 per cent). Sex work was usually viewed as 'work' (63 per cent) and less often as 'something I do when desperate for money' (22 per cent) or as a matter of survival (19 per cent). Like the female workers, males typically viewed those to whom they provided sex services as clients.

For the male sex workers who took part in the study, these clients were predominantly male. Like the female sex workers, male workers described their clients as coming from a diversity of occupational categories.

Despite these basic similarities, our study, as well as work conducted by others (e.g. Gilbert, 1996; Prestage, 1994; Waldorf and Murphy, 1990), would suggest that the experience of male sex workers differs in some important respects from that of female workers. Gilbert (1996) argues that male sex workers carry a triple stigma. As well as the stigma associated with sex work, there is also the stigma associated with homosexuality and AIDS. Overall, the indication is that male sex workers are exposed to levels of risk which are at least as great as, and probably even greater than, those faced by female sex workers.

Work locations of male sex workers

Male sex workers operated from work locations which were markedly different from those of most female workers ($p < 0.001$). In particular, relatively few males worked from organised settings, and only escort agencies appeared to employ male workers. As Table 10.1 shows, none of the males worked from massage parlours or parlour escort agencies, although these work settings accounted for some 40 per cent of female workers. Our data indicated that this difference was largely offset by the higher percentage of males working from the street. While relatively uncommon among female workers, street work, which may include work from specific locations such as gay bars, appeared to be fairly standard practice for male sex workers. As borne out in earlier sections of this report, when compared with other organised work settings, street work is likely to be associated with higher levels of physical and health-related risks.

Table 10.1
Current work location of 28 male and 200 female sex workers

	Males %	Females %
Massage parlour/brothel	0	16
Parlour escort	0	24
Escort agency	39	29
Street	36	6
Private	25	27

The above differences also applied to the settings from which male workers started work in the sex industry ($p < 0.001$). Table 10.2 shows that 57 per cent of males, compared with 12 per cent of females, started work on the street. Again relatively few males started work in an organised setting (escort agency), although such settings (massage parlour/brothel or escort agency) were typically the point of entry to the sex industry for females.

Table 10.2
Location in which 28 male and 200 female sex workers began work

	Males %	Females %
Massage parlour or brothel	0	41
Parlour escort	36	37
Escort agency	4	7
Street	57	12
Private	4	4

Workloads of male sex workers

The survey data suggested that males were more likely than females to use sex work as a supplement to some other form of income. While the majority of female workers (85 per cent) reported deriving all or most of their income from sex work, this was true for slightly less than half the males (46 per cent). These apparent workload differentials are illustrated further in Tables 10.3 and 10.4 which compare the number of clients seen by male and female workers and their earnings during the last week.

Most (85 per cent) of the male workers interviewed saw no more than 10 clients in the week preceding the interview which, according to the majority of the sample had been a typical week. Even during their 'busiest week', less than half the male workers (43 per cent) reported that they would see more than 10 clients. By contrast, 60 per cent of the female workers reported having provided services to more than 10 clients in the previous week.

Consistent with this, male sex workers tended to be concentrated in the lower income categories (Table 10.4). Based on this small group of male workers, our data suggested that females were earning a weekly average income double that of males ($p < 0.01$). This largely reflected the differing workloads in that, on a weekly basis, female sex workers averaged about twice as many clients as male sex workers ($p < 0.001$). When one examines the approximate income received per client service then the average fee received per service was similar for male and female workers.

Table 10.3
Number of clients seen by 28 male and 200 female sex workers

	Last week		Busiest week	
	Males %	Females %	Males %	Females %
0 to 5	64	15	32	5
6 to 10	21	27	25	9
11 to 15	4	25	11	11
16 to 20	7	21	18	24
> 20	4	14	14	52

Table 10.4
Earnings in the last seven days for 19 male and 170 female sex workers*

	Males $	Females $
Mean income	484	1110
Mean number of clients	6	15
Mean income per client	88	85

* Excludes workers who had no clients or no income in the last week and those who completed the pilot questionnaire

Entering the Industry

Table 10.5 compares male and female sex workers in terms of selected background characteristics. Most striking is the younger age at which the male sex workers had entered the industry ($p = 0.002$). In the present sample, almost three quarters of the men (71 per cent) had begun work in the sex industry before age 20, and all but one (96 per cent) had begun work by age 29. Far fewer women (38 per cent) had started work in the sex industry before age 20 and it was not uncommon (14 per cent) for women to have entered the industry aged 30 or older.

Nonetheless, the distributions of male and female workers according to length of time in the sex industry were very similar, the majority of both males and females having worked for two to nine years. Consistent with the younger age of entry to the industry, the males were a slightly (but not significantly) younger group.

Table 10.5
Comparison of male and female workers on selected worker characteristics

Worker characteristic	Males* %	Females* %
Aged 20-29 years	69	56
Worked 2-9 years	64	52
< 20 years when started	71	38
Single (never married)	85	57
Left school at less than 15 years	17	12
Left home at less than 15 years	11	8
Would like to leave sex industry	46	29

* N ranges from 19 to 28 (males) and from 197 to 200 (females)

Most (85 per cent) of the male workers who took part in the study described themselves as single, but a small number (15 per cent) were living with a partner. The male and female workers in the present sample did not differ in terms of the age at which they had left home or school and relatively few male or female workers had left home or school before the age of 15 years.

Almost half (46 per cent) the male sex workers stated that they would like to leave the sex industry. This figure is slightly higher than that observed for the female workers, but the main reasons given by males for not leaving – that they needed the money (69 per cent) and/or did not believe they could get any other form of work (43 per cent) – were similar.

The male and female groups tended to differ in terms of employment prior to becoming a sex worker (Table 10.6). Like the women, many males were unemployed when they entered the sex industry but one third described themselves as students at the time they entered the sex industry, compared with only 4 per cent of the women.

Table 10.6
Prior employment of 28 male and 200 female sex workers

Worker characteristic	Males %	Females %
Not employed	36	46
Student	32	4
Full-time employment	25	34
Part-time employment	7	8
Casual employment	0	3
Home duties	0	7

Knowledge and attitudes in relation to HIV/AIDS

Like the female sex workers, only the minority of male workers (25 per cent) considered that they had a greater than small risk of contracting HIV/AIDS. Consistent with this, the male workers as a group, did not appear to exhibit high levels of anxiety about becoming infected with HIV. Just over one third (39 per cent) reported being moderately or very anxious about the possibility.

Responses to an open-ended question indicated that, in most cases (86 per cent), male workers considered their risk of contracting HIV/AIDS to be small because they always used condoms. A strong belief in the high level of protection against AIDS offered by condoms is demonstrated in Table 10.7. Almost all (96 per cent) of the male workers acknowledged a high level of risk of HIV transmission associated with non-condom anal sex. However, most (85 per cent) considered the risk of transmission through anal sex to be only minimal if condoms were used and almost half (46 per cent) thought there was no risk. A similar pattern was evident for oral sex in that, with the proper use of condoms, most male workers (93 per cent) believed there was little or no risk attached to this practice. However, even without the use of condoms, many (40 per cent) considered oral sex to be relatively low risk.

The level of knowledge held by male sex workers about basic HIV/AIDS-related issues appeared very similar to that of female workers. Thus, most males (89 per cent) thought it impossible to tell by appearances if a person had AIDS, at least until the last stages of the disease. Similarly, all knew there was no cure or vaccine for AIDS and were aware of the meaning of a positive HIV test result.

Table 10.7
Perceived risk of HIV transmission among 28 male sex workers

	Without condoms			
	None %	Slight %	Moderate %	High %
Oral sex	11	29	18	43
Anal sex	0	0	4	96
Vaginal sex	0	0	18	82

	With proper use of condoms			
	None %	Slight %	Moderate %	High %
Oral sex	68	25	0	7
Anal sex	46	39	7	7
Vaginal sex	48	41	4	7

However, as in the case of female workers, some confusion was evident regarding the period of sero-conversion. Most male workers (86 per cent) responded that a negative HIV test result meant they were not infected but only 14 per cent indicated an understanding that this referred to their HIV status six to eight weeks ago. The majority (61 per cent) thought it would take some months before infection could be ruled out for certain following possible exposure to HIV but some thought infection could be excluded sooner (32 per cent) or did not know (7 per cent). Like the women, many (36 per cent) did not know how long the virus could live outside the body.

Services offered by male sex workers

Information about the types of services offered to clients by male sex workers is shown in Tables 10.8 and 10.9. These data are only available for 20 male workers and therefore provide only a broad indication of the range and availability of services. Nonetheless, it does appear that certain services are offered almost universally by male sex workers. These include anal sex, hand relief, and oral sex, performed by and on the worker. Some services such as massage and fantasy appear to be offered much less often by male than female workers. Conversely, anal sex, rimming, and fisting are offered far more often by male than female workers.

Table 10.8
Services provided for male clients by 20 male and 179 female sex workers

	Provide service		Use condom always	
	Males %	Females %	Males %	Females %
Oral sex with ejaculation	90	79	56	86
Oral sex no ejaculation	95	97	37	77
Oral sex (from male)	95	68	37	NA
Anal sex	90	12	89	90
Hand relief	95	98	5	15
Fisting	15	1	100	100
Rimming	40	0	50	NA
Fingering	15	21	0	31
Sex toys	20	40	100	93

NA = Not applicable

Table 10.9
Other services provided by 20 male and 179 female sex workers

	Males %	Females %
Massage	20	82
Golden showers	10	30
Bondage	25	24
Submission	0	4
Cross dressing	15	20
Fantasy	15	45

While most (89 per cent) of the male workers who provide anal sex stated that they always used condoms for this practice, condoms appeared to be used far less consistently for other commonly offered services. There is also some suggestion that male workers may use condoms less often than female workers. For instance, while 86 per cent of women reported always using condoms for oral sex with ejaculation, only 56 per cent of men did so.

Male workers, like their female counterparts, appeared rarely to use condoms when providing hand relief, usually because they thought they were unnecessary. By contrast, for anal sex, none of the male workers believed condoms were unnecessary. The small number of males who did not always use condoms said this was so because, on occasions, the client paid more or condoms were unavailable. In the case of oral sex, some of those male workers who did not always use condoms were paid more for not using condoms (28 per cent) while others thought they were unnecessary (28 per cent).

Other work-related health risks

Table 10.10 examines a number of work-related factors relevant to the risk of transmission of STDs and HIV/AIDS. Overall, these data suggest that male sex workers may well be exposed to a greater degree of risk than their female counterparts.

Table 10.10
Comparison of male and female workers on selected work-related variables

	Males* %	Females* %
Financial inducement for non-condom sex (at least weekly)	50	69
Condoms never break	37	38
Difficult to persuade clients to use condoms (at least sometimes)	33	16
Clients known to use injecting drugs	44	17
Check clients for STDs (always)	61	89
Have seen STDs on clients	64	68

* N ranges from 19 to 28 (males) and from 197 to 200 (females)

While the majority of male workers (61 per cent) reported always checking their clients for STDs, they may be less likely to do so than female workers (89 per cent). Male workers who checked clients for STDs had usually been shown by another worker (32 per cent) or had read about it (18 per cent). While relatively few female sex workers reported receiving any formal instruction from health professionals on how to check for STDs, such instruction appears to be virtually non-existent for male workers. Similar proportions of male (64 per cent) and female (68 per cent) workers reported having been exposed to clients who appeared to have an STD.

Half the males in the sample reported being offered a higher fee for non-condom sex at least once in an average week. This percentage is lower than that for female workers but given the smaller number of work-related sexual encounters for males (Table 10.3 suggests that female workers may see twice as many clients as male workers in a given week), on a per client basis, the frequency with which male workers are offered financial inducement is probably as high. Condom breakage must also be considered, particularly in view of the very high reliance placed on condom use. Only 37 per cent of male workers said they had never experienced condom breakage, a figure which is closely comparable to that reported by women.

Our data also suggested that males may have greater difficulty than females in persuading clients to use condoms and that they may see a greater proportion of clients who use injecting drugs. One third of male workers in the study reported having difficulty persuading clients to use condoms and almost half saw clients who are injecting drug users.

Non-work health risks

In their personal lives, male sex workers also appear to be exposed to risks that are at least as great as those for female workers (Table 10.11). Just over half the sample (54 per cent) of male workers reported having injected a drug or other substance. This rate is more than twice that reported by the female workers and is likely to far exceed that of many other groups within the general population. Of the 15 male workers who had ever injected a substance, many (73 per cent) had shared drug-taking equipment, and several (20 per cent) had done so within the last year.

Table 10.11
Comparison of male and female workers on selected non-work variables

	Males* %	Females* %
Ever injected a drug or other substance	54	23
Regular non-work sex partner	38	55
One or more other casual non-work sex partners (last year)	43	38
Use condoms all the time with regular partner	50	18

* N ranges from 19 to 28 (males) and from 196 to 200 (females)

Male and female workers were equally likely to have a regular non-work sex partner. Of 10 male sex workers (36 per cent) with a regular sex partner, six had a male and four a female partner. About half the male workers with a regular sex partner used condoms all the time with that partner. This was the case for only 18 per cent of female workers (with a male partner). Most (70 per cent) knew that their partner had had sex with other people and some (40 per cent) knew that he or she had injected a drug during the last year. Male and female workers were equally likely to report having had sex with one or more casual (non-work) partners during the year prior to the interview. While these numbers are very small and only trends can be noted, the data provide reason to expect that, like female workers, a sizeable proportion of male sex workers are likely to engage in or be exposed to high-risk activities in their private lives.

Health service utilisation

Most of the male sex workers (86 per cent) involved in the study had consulted a medical service during the previous year. Like the female workers, general practitioners were most frequently consulted for general health concerns (71 per cent) or STD checks (39 per cent). Most (78 per cent) of the male sex workers expressed satisfaction with available services.

Patterns of attendance for STD check-ups (Table 10.12) indicated that male workers had such checks less regularly than female workers ($p < 0.001$). Twenty-five per cent of male workers, compared with 3 per cent of female workers, reported never having STD checks. Consistent with the work locations of the males in the study, medical certificates were rarely (8 per cent) a work requirement.

Table 10.12
Frequency of STD checks for 28 male and 194 female workers

	Males %	Females %
At least monthly	14	38
Every 2 to 3 months	50	41
Once or twice a year	11	17
Never	25	3

Just over three quarters (79 per cent) of the male workers had been tested for HIV infection. This compared with 96 per cent of female workers and suggested that testing among male workers may have been less widespread than among female workers at the time the study was conducted ($p < 0.01$). The males who reported having been tested for HIV infection, had usually attended a general practioner (50 per cent) or STD clinic (45 per cent) for testing. Patterns of frequency of testing were broadly similar for male and female workers (Table 10.13). In both groups, the majority reported being tested on a three to six monthly basis while small minorities were not regularly tested for HIV. None of the male workers reported ever having received a positive test result.

Table 10.13
Frequency of HIV testing for 23 male and 189 female workers

	Males %	Females %
Every 1 to 2 months	9	28
Every 3 to 6 months	78	59
Every 1 to 2 years	4	8
Don't have the test regularly	9	5

Alcohol and drug use

As a group, male sex workers have high usage rates of a variety of legal and illegal substances (Tables 10.14 and 10.15). However, as was the case with the female workers, the present data are only broad indicators and do not provide details regarding the level or frequency of use.

Table 10.14
Legal substance use by 27 male sex workers

	Ever used %	Used last week %
Tobacco	85	85
Alcohol	85	81
Tranquillisers	19	15
Pain killers	7	7
Anti-depressants	4	4

Table 10.15
Illegal substance use by 27 male sex workers

	Ever used %	Used last week %
Cannabis	85	70
Heroin	48	7
Amphetamines	41	11
Ecstasy	22	7
Hallucinogens	19	-
Methadone	15	7
Cocaine	15	4
Barbiturates	4	4
Inhalants (e.g. glue)	4	4

The large majority of male workers had used alcohol and tobacco. Notably, cannabis use (70 per cent) seemed to be almost as prevalent as alcohol (81 per cent) and tobacco (85 per cent) use in the week before the study interview. Almost half the male workers had used heroin but only 7 per cent had done so in the last week. Similar numbers reported using amphetamines while smaller numbers had used a variety of other illicit drugs.

Slightly less than half the male workers (42 per cent) reported having sought treatment for a drug problem, a rate higher than that reported by female workers (15 per cent). Like the female workers, the drug most often involved was heroin. While 30 per cent of the males stated that their use of substances had increased since entering the industry, 62 per cent reported that it had remained unchanged.

Legal issues

Fifty per cent of the male workers reported having had no involvement with police during the last twelve months. Those who had been involved with the police were divided in terms of whether they described their dealings with police in a favourable or unfavourable way. These patterns were closely comparable to patterns of police involvement reported by the female workers. Our data suggested, however, that male workers may be more likely to be charged with offences related to sex work. One in three of the male workers had been charged on at least one occasion compared with about one in eight female workers ($p < 0.01$).

The data also suggested that male sex workers may be even less likely than female workers to report offences to police. Only 27 to 35 per cent stated that they would definitely report assault, rape or robbery perpetrated by a client or partner to the police. These figures are somewhat lower than the 54 to 58 per cent of women who stated they would report the same offences to police. The reasons given by male workers for not reporting offences were similar to those given by female workers: they did not want to bring themselves to police attention and/or did not think their complaint would be taken seriously.

About one third (32 per cent) of the male sex workers had been raped on at least one occasion and slightly more (46 per cent) reported having been bashed. These rates are comparable to those reported by the female sex workers, of whom 29 per cent had ever been raped and 30 per cent had ever been bashed. (For both males and females, these figures are not confined to the period during which the worker has been in the sex industry, but also include any earlier assaults). Sexual and other violence therefore appears to be no less prevalent among male sex workers and, as noted, they may be even less likely to report it than female workers.

Education, training and support

Like the female sex workers, most male workers (88 per cent) believed a need existed for formal training, covering such aspects as how to do STD checks, how to use condoms, sexual services, and negotiation with clients, before commencing work in the sex industry. When asked to rank a range of issues in terms of personal importance, most male workers (72 per cent) placed health among their top three priorities, followed by financial (57 per cent) and personal or social (47 per cent) issues.

Although male sex workers are likely to be a more marginalised group than female workers, almost all (96 per cent) had heard of SQWISI. Given SQWISI's role in recruiting workers to the study, it is likely that subgroups of workers not included in this study would have no knowledge of or contact with SQWISI. As was the case with the female workers, they had first heard of the organisation from a friend (56 per cent) more often than through formal channels. Half of the male workers in the study were members of SQWISI and 43 per cent received the organisation's regular publication. A small number of male workers (21 per cent) were SQWISI volunteers but, other than this, only in isolated cases had any formal contact (for example, workshop attendance, counselling) been made with the organisation.

Male workers (32 per cent) seemed less likely than female workers (81 per cent) to consider themselves a source of information for clients. Despite this, they appeared generally receptive to the notion of written material (50 per cent) and educational programs (25 per cent) to facilitate client education.

Like the female workers, males most often (44 per cent) considered SQWISI the best source of information on STDs and HIV/AIDS. Books (31 per cent) were the next most popular source of information for male workers, followed by STD clinics (22 per cent), doctors (18 per cent) and the AIDS Council (18 per cent).

This is in some contrast to the female workers who frequently nominated doctors (41 per cent) as the best source of information. Overall, most male workers thought there was enough information available on STDs and HIV/AIDS but a small number (17 per cent) thought the available information was inadequate.

Most (85 per cent) male workers thought special programs should be available to help people leave the industry if they wished and 50 per cent indicated that they themselves would be interested in participating in such a program. In terms of assistance with leaving the industry, 57 per cent to 64 per cent of male workers nominated the following: financial help, personal counselling, drug and alcohol counselling or treatment and access to training courses and special study grants.

Summary

Male sex workers are likely to represent a small and marginalised group, who are at high risk for a range of adverse health outcomes. Despite the small numbers on which our results are based, there is reason to suspect that male sex workers are exposed to and engage in a range of practices that place them at even higher risk than their female counterparts. Indeed, as a group, they tend to resemble the female street workers who, as shown earlier, appear to be at greater risk than other female sex workers.

11 Conclusions

This report has examined a range of issues related to sex work and HIV/AIDS as well as other factors of significance in sex workers' lives. The experiences reported in the course of this study support Neave's (1988) argument that attempts to suppress prostitution of one type or in one geographical area simply cause it to increase in other forms or locations. The organisation of prostitution in Queensland has no doubt changed since the data were collected for this study but many of the realities for workers within the various types of prostitution settings are likely to remain valid.

Self reports of HIV status indicated that no workers in the sample were HIV positive. This is consistent with other reports of HIV status among sex workers in Australia. However, as the potential for infection is unknown, the high level of condom use apparently adopted by Queensland sex workers is likely to have made a significant contribution. Only a small proportion of workers did not insist on condoms for sex practices known to be associated with a higher risk of transmission.

Street workers and male workers are at particularly high risk and the importance of outreach to these more marginalised groups is clearly indicated. Given the changing nature of the sex industry and the settings from which workers operate, particularly in response to legislative changes enforced since the completion of this survey, there is a need to monitor the impact of these changes on sex worker health.

Despite considerable effort by the research team, 'street kids' and workers from Asian parlours were not recruited to this study. Further work is needed to explore issues around prostitution for both these groups. Although street kids engage in the exchange of sex for money or goods, they do not appear to define this as prostitution and operate quite separately from the commercial sex industry. This separation is significant as stereotypes of the commercial sex industry are often based on the assumption that those in the industry prey upon and recruit the vulnerable and homeless and that under-age and child prostitution is flourishing within the commercial sex industry. Our study however, found only 4 per cent of workers began work at less than 15 years of age and at the time of our study only 3 per cent of the sample were under 18. The issue of child sexual abuse is, of course, of major concern but it should not be confused with the commercial sex industry.

In relation to workers in Asian parlours, the few interviews which were obtained suggest major problems of exploitation, high risk practices, violence, isolation and little control for sex workers. Again they operate separately from the 'mainstream' commercial industry and require careful and sensitive approaches to investigations in this area.

The importance of condom use should continue to be promoted for the protection of both workers and their clients. Education should continue to stress the use of condoms as the most effective method of protection for all sexual activity, and that STD checks in themselves do not contribute to a reduction in HIV risk as perceived by some workers.

For a small group of women the assumption that certain practices, including vaginal sex, are low risk may result in condoms not being used because they are not considered necessary. Pressure from clients, including financial incentives, not to use a condom may increase this likelihood.

A high level of knowledge about HIV transmission and risk practices was evident. However, some knowledge gaps among workers indicate that education programs need to emphasise:

- withdrawing before ejaculation can still be risky;
- the potential for transmission through contact between broken skin and blood or semen;
- the possibility of a mother passing the virus to her baby during pregnancy and breast feeding; and
- the high level of safety of blood transfusions and haemophiliac treatment.

Further education is also needed regarding HIV testing, particularly with regard to the sero-conversion period following infection. A significant number of workers thought that HIV infection could be detected much sooner than is in fact possible following unsafe sexual contact with an infected person. Education needs to clarify the stages of HIV infection and the link with developing AIDS-related symptoms.

Checking clients for physical symptoms of STDs is practised by the majority of workers and should continue to be promoted. This is not so much because of its value as a preventive practice (many STDs are not always visible), but rather it may assist in ensuring that the worker is sensitive to the risk of an STD and in charge of the negotiation of safe sex.

Education about health risks associated with clients is essential for workers. They need to be advised not to have sex with clients where any signs of STDs are present but to offer alternative services. In this respect, their level of awareness of risks associated with client intravenous drug use needs also to be increased. A need for knowledge of referral agencies for clients is also indicated.

Most workers are responsible for putting the condom on their client. Educational messages need to stress the correct use of condoms and skills which some workers have acquired in putting condoms on clients as part of the sexual repertoire should be promoted. The use of lubricant should be promoted as part of safe sex and particularly as a means of preventing condom breakage.

Practitioners of Bondage and Discipline services need education about the risk of infection from equipment used in these practices. Equipment such as whips, dildos and sharp instruments such as knives, scalpels and needles need adequate sterilisation between use.

Education on contraceptive methods needs to be promoted. Our data suggest that the use of contraception is not widespread among workers.

A significant proportion of sex workers' clients are regulars. This has implications for the education of clients in that safe sex messages could be repeated and reinforced with the same client over several visits. Supporting pictorial educational materials need also to be made available to workers for this purpose. The development of education programs for clients generally and appropriate printed informational materials in particular are also recommended for workers who agree to undertake a role as client educators.

Ideally, new workers would receive formal training from experienced workers with ongoing support and reinforcement from a peer-based organisation such as SQWISI. Management should take responsibility for the adequate induction of new workers focusing on safe sex and negotiation with clients. Management should also promote and support safe sex through formal policies which are made clear to clients. However, the current legal situation in Queensland is such that structures which allow this approach are illegal.

Workers face a number of pressures not to practice safe sex on a regular basis. Education and peer support play an important role in initiating and maintaining safe behaviour. The negotiation with the client about condom use is a particularly sensitive issue and learning appropriate skills is an important part of promoting preventive practices among new workers. Peer education to encourage and assist workers in negotiating with clients about condoms is recommended, again as new workers are being introduced to the work.

Other health service providers, especially general practitioners and STD clinic staff, who provide the bulk of sexual health services to workers in the sex industry need also to be aware of pertinent issues for sex workers.

Sex worker education also presents an opportunity to address risk practices with sex partners in workers' private lives. Sensitivity is needed to acknowledge the more personal nature of the relationships with private partners and the specific meaning placed on the use of the condom as separating work from private relationships. Skills training in safe sex negotiation with private partners should draw on models adopted for use in the general community.

Other areas which would seem to warrant consideration are cigarette, alcohol and other drug use, re-training options and issues related to financial planning. Substance use (particularly cigarette use) is very high in this group and such behaviours need to be understood and addressed.

The key findings of this study largely support previous research, inquiries and reports which indicate that HIV transmission in the commercial sex industry in Australia is likely to be minimal given current levels of protective behaviours. Specific groups of workers, such as males, street workers and occupationally isolated workers, require special approaches to ensure that this record is maintained. Opportunities to provide such assistance may be hampered by the current legislation.

Our study found that while most female workers began in massage parlours the younger workers in our study were more likely to have started in escort or street work. With the legislation change and subsequent closure of many parlours, this trend is likely to have increased.

Overall, our findings would suggest that the picture for workers who choose to work within the narrow legal framework established in Queensland is one of isolated and untrained workers operating from less safe environments, with some workers perhaps engaging in practices that place them at heightened risk for HIV infection. Workers must choose between this option (if they have the personal and financial skills and resources to establish it) and an illegal environment. Many workers will continue to choose the latter where, even though they might be at risk of prosecution, involvement with drugs and organised crime, they at least feel safe from attack, invisible and able to work.

References

Allen, J. (1984), The making of a prostitute proleteriat in early twentieth century New South Wales. In K. Daniels (ed.), *So much hard work: Women and prostitution in Australian history*, Fontana/Collins, Sydney.

Anderson, K. (1991), The process of change in Queensland: A worker's perspective. Paper presented at *Sex Industry and Public Policy Conference*, Canberra.

Australian Bureau of Statistics (1992), *1989-90 National Health Survey Health Risk Factors, Queensland*. Commonwealth of Australia, Canberra.

Australian Capital Territory (1991), *Interim Report of the Select Committee on HIV, Illegal Drugs and Prostitution*, Legislative Assembly, Canberra.

Banach, L. (1992), *Sex workers experiences of the impact of the law on their daily lives: A qualitative study*. Unpublished thesis, The University of Queensland.

Baxter, J., Emmison, M., Western, J. and Western, M. (1991), *Class Analysis and Contemporary Australia*. Macmillan, Melbourne.

Boyle, F.M., Dunne, M. P., Najman, J. M., Western, J. S., Turrell, G., Wood, C. and Glennon, S. (in press), Psychological distress among female sex workers. *Australian and New Zealand Journal of Public Health*.

Collaery, B. (1991), The sex industry in the ACT: A law reformer's perspective. Paper presented at *Sex Industry and Public Policy Conference*, Canberra.

Commonwealth Department of Health, Housing, Local Government and Community Services (1993), *Drug use and exposure in the Australian community*. Commonwealth of Australia, Canberra.

Criminal Justice Commission (1991), *Regulating Morality? An Inquiry into Prostitution in Queensland*. Report of the Criminal Justice Commission, September 1991.

Day, S. (1988), Prostitute women and AIDS: Anthropology, *AIDS*, 2(6), 421-428.

Day, S. and Ward, H. (1990), The Praed Street Project: A cohort of prostitute women in London. In M. Plant (ed.), *AIDS, drugs, and prostitution*. Routledge, London.

De Graaf, R., Vanwesenbeeck, I., van Zessen, G., Straver, C.J. and Visser, J.H. (1995), Alcohol and drug use in heterosexual and homosexual prostitution, and its relation to protection behvaiour, *AIDS Care*, 7 (1), 35-47.

Donovan, B. (1990), Female sex workers in Australia: So far so good. *National AIDS Bulletin*, 4(5), 17.

Dorfman, L.E., Derish, P.A. and Cohen, J.B. (1992), Hey girlfriend: An evaluation of AIDS prevention among women in the sex industry. *Health Education Quarterly*, 19(1), 25-40.

Elifson, K., Boles, J. and Sweat, M. (1993), Risk factors associated with HIV injection among male prostitutes. *American Journal of Public Health*, 83(1), 79-83.

Estebanez, P., Fitch, K. and Najera, R. (1993), HIV and female sex workers. *Bulletin of the World Health Organization*, 71(3/4), 397-412.

Feacham, R.J.A. (1995), *Valuing the past investing in the future. Evaluation of the National HIV/AIDS Strategy 1993-94*. Australian Government Publishing Service, Canberra.

Fisher, G.D. (1988), Possible effects of reference group-based social influence on AIDS-risk behaviour and AIDS prevention. *American Psychologist*, 43, 914-920.

Gilbert, K. (1996), Boys to men, *National AIDS Bulletin*, 10 (5), 16-17.

Goldberg, D. and Williams, P. (1988), *A users guide to the General Health Questionnaire*, NFER-Nelson, Windsor, Berkshire.

Griggs, L. and Alan, D. (1990), Male sex workers and HIV in Sydney: A potted history. *National AIDS Bulletin*, 4(5), 20-21.

Harcourt, C. (1994), Prostitution and public health in the era of AIDS, In R. Perkins, G. Prestage, R. Sharp and F. Lovejoy (eds.), *Sex work and sex workers in Australia*, University of New South Wales Press, Sydney.

Harcourt, C. and Philpot, R. (1990), Female prostitutes, AIDS, drugs, and alcohol in New South Wales. In M. Plant (ed.), *AIDS, drugs, and prostitution*. Routledge, London.

Hatty, S. (1991), The desired object: Prostitution in Canada, United States and Australia. Paper presented at *Sex Industry and Public Policy Conference*, Canberra.

Hobson, B.M. (1987), *Uneasy virtue: The politics of prostitution and the American reform tradition*. Basic Books Inc., New York.

Hunter, A. (1991), The development of theoretical approaches to sex work in Australian Sex Worker Rights Groups. Paper presented at *Sex Industry and Public Policy Conference*, Canberra.

Jackson, L., Highcrest, A. and Coates, R. A. (1992), Varied potential risks of HIV infection among prostitutes, *Social Science and Medicine*, 35 (3), 281-286.

Kinsey, A.L., Pomeroy, W.B. and Martin, C.E. (1948), *Sexual behavior in the human male*, Saunders, Philadelphia.

Leonardo, C. and Chrisler, J.C. (1992), Women and sexually transmitted diseases. *Women and Health*, 18(4), 1-15.

National Drug Strategy (1993), *1993 National Drug Household Survey*. Australian Government Publishing Service, Canberra (Queensland data supplied by Alcohol and Drug Branch, Queensland Health).

Neave, M. (1988), The failure of prostitution law reform: The Fifteenth Annual John Barry Memorial Lecture, *Australian and New Zealand Journal of Criminology*, 21(4), 203-213.

Pascoe, G.C. (1983), Patient satisfaction in primary health care: A literature review and analysis. *Evaluation and Program Planning*, 6, 185-210.

Perkins, R. (1994), Female prostitution. In R. Perkins, G. Prestage, R. Sharp and F. Lovejoy (eds.), *Sex work and sex workers in Australia*, University of New South Wales Press, Sydney.

Perkins, R., Lovejoy, F. and Jacobsen, M. (1996), Clients of sex workers: sexual behaviour and safe sex practices, *National AIDS Bulletin*, 10 (5), 28-31.

Perkins, R., Prestage, G., Sharp, R. and Lovejoy, F. (eds.) (1994), *Sex work and sex workers in Australia*, University of New South Wales Press, Sydney.

Plant, M. (ed.) (1990), *AIDS, drugs, and prostitution*. Routledge, London.

Prestage, G. (1994), Male and transsexual prostitution. In R. Perkins, G. Prestage, R. Sharp and F. Lovejoy (eds.), *Sex work and sex workers in Australia*, University of New South Wales Press, Sydney.

Pyett, P.M. and Warr, D.J. (1996), *When 'gut instinct' is not enough: Women at risk in sex work*. Centre for the Study of Sexually Transmissible Diseases, La Trobe University, Melbourne.

Select Committee on HIV, Illegal Drugs and Prostitution (1991), *Prostitution in the ACT*, Interim report, April 1991.

Seng, M.J. (1989), Child sexual abuse and adolescent prostitution: A comparative analysis. *Adolescence*, XXIV (95), 665-675.

Smart, C. (1976), Women crime and criminology: A feminist critique. Routledge and Kegan Paul, London.

Stevens, C. (1994), AIDS education and prevention strategies in the sex industry. In R. Perkins, G. Prestage, R. Sharp and F. Lovejoy (eds.), *Sex work and sex workers in Australia*, University of New South Wales Press, Sydney.

Sullivan, B. (1991), Feminist perspective to clarify the issues of the sex industry. Paper presented at *Sex Industry and Public Policy Conference*, Canberra.

Summers, A. (1975), *Damned whores and God's police: The colonization of women in Australia*, Allen Lane, London.

Victorian Inquiry into Prostitution (1985), Report on Inquiry into Prostitution. Victorian Government, Melbourne.

Waldorf, D. and Murphy, S. (1990), Intravenous drug use and syringe-sharing practices of call men and hustlers. In M. Plant (ed.), *AIDS, drugs, and prostitution*, Routledge, London.

Wilson, D. (1988), *Survey of Queenslanders' Attitudes to AIDS*. Report prepared for Queensland Department of Health.

Wilson, P. and Arnold, J. (1986), *Street kids: Australia's alienated young*. Collins Dove, Blackburn.

Yew, L. and Need, J.A. (1988), Women's health needs. *The Medical Journal of Australia*, 148, 110-112.

Zajdow, G. (1991), Sex work and regulation: Holding onto an image. Paper presented at *Sex Industry and Public Policy Conference*, Canberra.